SWEET SORROW

SWEET SORROW
Love, Loss and Attachment
in Human Life

Alan B. Eppel

"Parting is such sweet sorrow"
Romeo & Juliet Act 2 Scene 2

KARNAC

First published in 2009 by
Karnac Books Ltd
118 Finchley Road
London NW3 5HT

British Library Cataloguing in Publication Data

A C.I.P. for this book is available from the British Library

ISBN-13: 978-1-85575-645-8

Typeset by Vikatan Publishing Solutions (p) Ltd., Chennai, India

www.karnacbooks.com

CONTENTS

PREFACE

Like most people, I did not learn everything in kindergarten. But I did learn something about attachment. It happened when I was four years old, on my first day at school. It was then that I first apprehended the rude shock of emotions that make up separation anxiety.

I somehow successfully persuaded my father that I did not need to stay and eagerly returned home to my waiting mother. She seemed a little surprised but unfazed to be told that the school was closed and that I didn't have to go that day.

I was first exposed to attachment theory during my psychiatry residency training at McMaster University in Hamilton Ontario. This was in the late seventies and indeed John Bowlby visited one year to talk about his theories. In 1977 two of his classical papers appeared in the British Journal of Psychiatry and a question on attachment appeared on the Royal College of Psychiatrists' Membership exam which I took the following year.

In those days Bowlby's ideas were vastly underappreciated in North America and it is only in the last decade that attachment theory has been recognized as central to understanding human psychology and neurobiology.

Following my psychiatric training I worked for a period at the Homewood Sanitarium in Guelph Ontario, a 200 bed psychiatric hospital and in the Arbors Day program also in Guelph. There we were faced with many patients, mostly young women but some men, who proved most difficult to treat. These patients appeared to be continuously suicidal and made frequent suicide attempts. They displayed intensely reactive moods of anger and dysphoria. They were extremely sensitive to rejection and to being alone. At that time the term "Borderline Personality" was just entering into the psychiatric vernacular. It was only in 1980 with the appearance of DSM 3 that it became an officially endorsed diagnostic entity. Consequently it took us some time to recognize these patients and to work out the best responses to their struggles. Paul Links at McMaster was undertaking some of the early studies of diagnostic stability of the BPD concept and I was fortunate to be able to collaborate with him and his colleagues Marilyn Korzekwa and Meir Steiner. It seemed to me then, as it does now, that the behaviour of people with borderline personality could best be understood using John Bowlby's Attachment theory. Over the ensuing thirty years since then, working with these patients and others with related problems, it has become apparent that people with so called borderline personality exhibit the conflicts and struggles that are universal to all human beings. It is through them and my other patients that I have learned so much about the human condition.

I have chosen to write this book in order to pass on what I have learned and experienced over these years. I have tried to develop a coherent philosophy by synthesising ideas from many sources of human knowledge and art. Certainly there is much that is speculative even provocative but I believe that each reader will be able to draw some words of wisdom and even inspiration from Sweet Sorrow.

I will start my acknowledgments with the usual humble disclaimer that any shortcomings of this book are attributable solely to the author and can in no way reflect on those who have assisted and advised me. I would therefore like to thank those who read parts of the manuscript and offered helpful feedback: Jenny Sheridan and David Abrahamson in London; Mossy Abrahamson in Dublin; my colleagues Anne Becker at Harvard, Mamta Gautam in Ottawa,

Eve Leeman from Columbia, Oonagh Zuberbier in Vancouver, Nora Jane Thormann in Porto Alegre, Anna K. Meyer in Seattle and Sarah McVanel here in Hamilton. Thanks also to Andrea McGuire who did most of the keyboarding. I extend my appreciation to the staff at Karnac for their helpfulness and expertise.

To my children and to those to whom they are attached, Ayelet, Joel, Noam, Aimee, Yonah and Amanda thank you for your love, your patience and encouragement. To Yonah also thanks for the skill and ideas you brought to the cover design. I hope you all will find some wisdom in this work.

Above all I wish to express my deepest gratitude and love to my wife Patricia Tolkin Eppel for her love, support, courage and generosity.

Alan Eppel Hamilton, Ontario 2008

INTRODUCTION

All of us seek to understand the meaning of life, and especially the meaning of our own lives. We struggle with the mysteries of birth and death, of love and loss. These are fundamental to our nature as human beings. But what drives us? What impels us on our daily round of tasks and relationships? What propels us forward in pursuit of what unclear purpose, what ill defined and hazy consummation?

In this volume I propose that it is the interplay of love and loss that lies at the epicentre of the human story. Support for this proposal will be taken from neuroscience, art and psychoanalysis. I will also introduce the reader to important ideas and findings from Attachment theory. An exploration of the relationship between love and loss can lead us to some understanding of the meaning of our lives. I hope to show how love and loss are inextricably bound at the centre of human experience, and form the essential dynamic of the human struggle.

The title of this volume, "*Sweet Sorrow*", may at first appear to be a contradiction. It is easy to understand Romeo and Juliet's sorrow when they are forced to part, but why is it "sweet"?

On reflection it becomes apparent that a parting is only sorrowful when the two people in question have a close or loving relationship. In fact this is self-evident and forms part of all our experiences. The more intense the attachment, that is the love between the couple, the more sorrowful the parting. In more concise terms the sweetness and sorrow are directly correlated with each other: more of one leads to more of the other. Juliet can only experience the sorrow if she has experienced the sweetness of the love.

Kahil Gibran (1923) expressed the same idea in *"The Prophet"*:

> "And ever has it been that love knows not its own depth until the hour of separation."

Unfortunately it is part of human life that separation and loss frequently follow periods of attachment. In fact inevitably *all attachments will come to an end*, whether through physical separation or death. Not a very comforting thought but one we must look square in the eye if we wish to uncover the enigma of our place in this world.

What is the nature of the relationship of loss to love? Why is it so central to our lives? How does it shape us? How does it determine our outlook and our behaviour? These are the motifs of this book.

Through this exploration I will demonstrate that answers to these questions emerge from our biology and our psychology. I will draw on scientific and artistic sources. The scientific sources include the fields of neuroscience and child development. Where these cannot assist us, the wisdom of psychoanalysis will be consulted. The status of psychoanalysis as a science has been debated since its inception. At the very least it provides us with a heuristic language; a language of rich metaphor and analogy; as yet we have no other medium to describe and conceptualise the workings of the human psyche.

I will also bring forth the wisdom of art which contains within it the origins of another sort of truth: art is a manifestation of man's inner feelings expressed in concrete form—as paintings, poems, and in cinema.

What we call 'love' can be regarded as the subjective component of a program of human behaviour known as "Attachment". Over three decades ago, John Bowlby developed his theory of Attachment, a theory as far-reaching in its impact as that of Sigmund Freud, fifty years earlier.

We live in an age where science and technology have clearly triumphed over other worldviews and dominate the discourse of our daily existence. The reader might then question why I have drawn so significantly from artistic sources. The great scientist and humanist Jacob Bronowki spent much of his life grappling with this question: Can art, particularly Poetry, convey universal truths in a way no less valid than the pursuit of knowledge through Science? He says:

> "I have no doubt now that there is a common quality in science and in poetry- the quality of imagination... the imagination reaches us, reaches into us , in different ways in science and in poetry. In science it organizes our experience into laws on which we can base our actions in the future. But poetry is another mode of knowledge, in which we become one with the poet and enter directly into his and into all human experience." (Bronowski, 1978, p. 4).

The same can be said for other forms of art, painting, photography, cinema, drama, and of course music. Each of the arts is associated with a different sense/perceptual modality: mainly visual or auditory. Painting, especially expressive painting, speaks directly to our own inner experiences and emotions.

Music has a unique place among the artistic forms. Music is the language of the limbic system; it is the language of our emotions and speaks directly to our emotions, bypassing the elaborate structure of our intellectual brain, the frontal neocortex. Poetry is related to music. It is also a rhythmic language that reaches deep into our emotional core.

It is quite startling to see how advances in neuroscience are consistent with the "poetic" wisdom we derive from the artistic works. The development of neuroimaging with MRI and PET scans has resulted in an understanding of the neurocircuits and chemistry underlying the experiences of our senses and affective life.

What this book is not about

"The most important things to do in the world are to get something to eat, something to drink and somebody to love you." **Brendan Behan**.

Brendan Behan, the famous Irish playwright and poet, shrewdly places food and water ahead of love, in his brief list of important priorities. He is correct in adducing that Love is not the pre-eminent human drive. It is preceded by the drives for self-preservation and survival. Maslow, in his universally famous theory, starts in the same place as Behan and describes a hierarchy of human needs:

Firstly there are **physiological needs**. The need for air, food and water. This implies freedom from famine and starvation.

The next level in Maslow's hierarchy are **safety and security needs** and arise when the physiological needs are largely taken care of. This includes a safe environment, and would therefore apply to freedom from war, and oppression; freedom from exposure to arbitrary arrest, detention, torture, and execution. It is only when these basic requirements are secured that there is the possibility for meaning at a level that can fulfil Maslow's **love and belonging needs**.

In our own times there are millions of people who live under threat of famine and deprivation; who are at continuous risk of death through war or environmental catastrophe. Certainly love and loss occur in dramatic and powerful ways in these societies also, but the consciousness of them is overshadowed by the urgent focus on preservation and survival.

This book will not address these societies but will focus on those fortunate enough to have the first two levels of Maslow's hierarchy reasonably and consistently met. By and large these are people who live under conditions of democracy and economic certainty and have the luxury of seeking higher levels of fulfilment, meaning and self-actualization (Maslow, 1970). Our discussion then starts at this point of reference, which in the course of history and geography has been the privilege of the minority.

This distinction between survival needs and love (as Attachment) may be somewhat arbitrary. Does the infant at birth seek attachment or food? Is it love or feeding that binds the infant to the mother? These questions take us immediately to a crucial divergence in the theories of Human Psychology. For Sigmund Freud the drive for food took precedence over the drive for care and affection. For the British School of psychoanalysis the drive for the other person was primordial. The British analyst W.R.D. Fairbairn famously expressed this as: "the Ego is Object seeking". Michael Balint would refer to this as " Primary Love".

This book is not about 'Spirituality' or 'Transcendence'. Rather it is rooted in our lived experiences, drawing from science and art. Below are eleven propositions. I will examine the basis for these by referring to work in infant development, psychology, psychoanalysis, and neurobiology. Supporting examples will be taken from cinema, music and art. As well, some clinical case studies will be introduced to illustrate important ideas. The case studies are composites and all identifying details have been removed.

Propositions to be considered:

Proposition #1 The drive to attach is fundamental and primary to human nature.

Proposition #2 Strivings for attachment are the strongest motivators of human behaviour.

Proposition #3 Identity is formed from interpersonal interaction, and emerges from the repeated interactions with the attachment figures.

Proposition #4a Mood is the bedrock of identity and the sense of self.

Proposition #4b Instability of mood gives rise to instability of the sense of Identity.

Proposition #5 Psychiatric disorders both reflect and affect the expression of love and loss.

Proposition #6 Disorders of sexual desire comprise the inability to maintain healthy attachments simultaneously with sexual intercourse.

Proposition #7 The intensity of loss and grief is directly proportional to the intensity of the attachment bond and its felt component, love.

Proposition #8 The death instinct exerts its effects when attachments are lost.

Proposition #9 Time is relative; acceleration of time is associated with alienation; expansion of time is associated with authentic human experience.

Proposition #10 The need for meaning is a fundamental property of human nature.

Proposition #11 The primary drive to attach gives rise to the strongest sense of meaning in human interaction.

CHAPTER ONE

Attachment

Proposition #1 The drive to attach is fundamental and primary to human nature.

The human infant commences life with an unwelcome propulsion from its mother's womb. The umbilical cord is quite literally and unceremoniously cut. The infant is for the first time separate from its mother. And it is here with this radical transforming event that I will begin our exploration of human nature.

One can imagine in early human environments and certainly in animal environments that there would be inherent dangers if the infant took it upon himself to venture forth into the world and lose contact with its mother. The mother is the provider of food and protection from predators. It was the British psychiatrist John Bowlby in his groundbreaking work, "*Attachment and Loss*", who put forth the concept of "Attachment". Attachment is an inborn biological drive within the infant that causes it to remain in close proximity to its mother. The impulse to attach is one of the most fundamental dimensions of human nature and consequently a fitting place to start our inquiry.

1

It is now well established that the attainment of secure attachment in childhood is essential for the normal development of the human infant. It provides the basis for the development of normal relationships with parents, siblings and eventually with a spouse or partner.

Attachment behaviour can be observed in all infants. It is characterized by a constant seeking to be in close proximity to the mother figure. Proximity seeking refers to the behaviours of the infant that bring it close to the mother. When the infant is separated or distant from the mother, there is a change in the infant's mood. It becomes distressed and this distress is signalled by vocalizations such as crying. This is "separation distress". With repeated interactions and positive responses from the mother or mother figure, the infant develops a sense that the mother is a constant figure. The mother has become a "secure base". Once a sense of a secure base has been established the infant then can begin to venture forth and explore his surroundings on his journey to increasing separateness and independence.

Psychoanalytic authors have referred to the close "symbiotic" tie between mother and infant in the early years of development. Margaret Mahler has described a developmental process which involves the infant moving from a state of symbiosis to one of

Photo: Christopher Gilbert

Figure 1. Attachment behaviour?

gradual increasing independence. During these early months and years of development, the infant is beginning to distinguish himself from the mother. Initially the boundary between "me" and "not me" is unclear. The infant has little awareness of where his body ends and that of the mother's begins. The growth of the brain results in advances in perception and cognition. The infant begins to form a sense and perhaps even a mental representation of himself as distinct from the mother figure. Nevertheless, moving away from the mother figure creates immense fear and anxiety and it is only with time that the infant begins to develop, in Winnicott's words, the "capacity to be alone".

Such sequences will be familiar to all who have watched young children develop. When the infant begins to crawl, in the early months of development, he may venture a certain distance from the mother frequently looking back over his shoulder to check that the mother is still there. With repetition and growth he acquires the secure feeling that the mother will remain in place. He is then able to venture further in his explorations of the environment. There is still a limit as to how far he will travel without returning back to the "home base" or the "secure base" represented by the mother figure. With further maturation and cognitive development, the infant attains the capacity to have an image of the mother internally represented within its mind. This permits the infant to move to places from where the mother is no longer in visual contact; the sense of security is now carried within or "internalized". This achievement is referred to as the acquisition of object constancy. It is a prerequisite for the individual in order to proceed to a normal level of independent functioning. Some people never acquire this object constancy and have problems throughout their lives with separation. More about this later.

The concept of attachment grew out of psychoanalytic thinking. Bowlby was a member of the British Group of Psychoanalysts, which included famously legendary figures such as Melanie Klein, Donald Winnicott, and Ronald Fairbairn. It was this British Object Relations school, expanding on some of Freud's earlier work, that proposed the idea of internalized representations of the outer world of relationships. And in fact, it was Fairbairn who proposed that the human animal is primarily "object seeking", meaning that there is a primary human drive to enter into relationships. This primary drive supersedes other needs such as the need for food or for sexual gratification. Experiments with monkeys carried out by Harlow provided some of the empirical support for this view. Harlow demonstrated that young monkeys preferred terry cloth mother figures over the wire figures that provided food. The young monkeys chose tactile warmth and soothing in preference to the mere provision of food by cold and uncomforting mother surrogates.

The evidence for attachment came initially out of research in ethology, the study of animal behaviour, and it was this major contribution that Bowlby brought to the psychiatric understanding of human nature. The precursors to this theory were more abstract and conceptual, based largely on the analysis and observations of adults. There were a limited number of direct observational studies of young children made by individual analysts. Melanie Klein and Anna Freud were early pioneers in working directly with children. More systematic studies were undertaken by Margaret Mahler's group.

The model of attachment has been well established in the psychiatric and psychological fields for some decades. More recently there have been striking breakthroughs in the understanding of attachment from a neurobiological point of view. This is in consequence of the enormous strides in neuroscience and neuroimaging.

A major contribution to this work has been made by Jaak Panksepp, a neuroscientist at Bowling Green State University in Ohio. Panksepp is one of the leading brain researchers of our day and has proposed that mammals have a specific neurocircuit that is the substrate for affiliation and attachment. He has also postulated that certain brain chemicals play a fundamental role in attachment behaviours, in particular, he has hypothesized that oxytocin, prolactin and the endogenous opioids play an important part in the instigation and regulation of attachment. Oxytocin is a hormone produced in the hypothalamus and it is involved in birth, breastfeeding and sexuality. Prolactin is produced in the pituitary gland and is instrumental in lactation.

Panksepp discovered that when an animal is separated from its mother and is experiencing separation distress, the administration of opiates (morphine-like chemicals) results in a reduction of the distress and the accompanying distress vocalizations. Most interestingly, the separation distress is potently inhibited by brain opioids that act at the mu opioid receptor. These are the same receptors that mediate addiction to morphine, heroin and other opiate drugs.

Panksepp also describes that touch activates the endogenous opioid system and this may be the basis for the positive soothing effects of touch. The hormones oxytocin and prolactin may also play a role in contact comfort. Drug abuse stimulates the same pathways that are involved in attachment behaviour. Brain chemicals that reduce separation distress promote social attachment and bonding. Specific areas of the brain appear to be involved in this process e.g. the cingulate cortex, the septal area, the orbital prefrontal cortex, and the amygdala.

There is evidence that the neurotransmitter serotonin modulates the separation response. Increased levels of serotonin reduce distress vocalizations in animals. This may explain some of the effects of medications in alleviating separation anxiety and related symptoms in psychiatric patients.

Serotonin stimulates the production and secretion of oxytocin and vasopressin in the hypothalamus. This interconnection between the serotonin and neuropeptide systems may have implications for psychiatric treatment.

Conversely, infant separation leads to changes in the pituitary-adrenal stress response that in turn depletes serotonin, norepinephrine and dopamine leading to the features of depression and despair.

Regulation of mood and brain development

Schore (2001) has proposed that the regulation of affect is a central organizing principle of human development and motivation. The first three years of life appear to be critical for the development of the right side of the brain. The maturation of the right brain, which includes frontal and limbic areas, depends on the nature and quality of the attachment relationship with the mother figure. Secure attachment leads to the healthy development of the right brain and optimal infant mental health. Conversely, traumatic attachment leads to impaired development of the right brain and a predisposition to mental illness.

This is really a very dramatic proposition: it has been here proposed that psychological events i.e. the quality of the interactions between the infant and the mother figure during the first three years of development, can actually impact the way the unfolding brain develops i.e. can lead to permanent alterations in the organization and functioning of the neurocircuits that underlie the regulation of emotion.

Schore further proposes that the quality of the attachment relationship influences the developing connections in the limbic system, which are involved in the regulation of affect. Schore points out that the mother and child synchronize the intensity of their affective interaction; there is a reciprocal response between eye gaze, facial expression and the rhythm and tempo of interaction. There is "a mutual empathic attunement". This synchrony may be essential for the development of healthy attachment and affect regulation. High quality attachment reduces negative affect (irritability, anger, fear, despair) and also amplifies positive emotions (contentment, satisfaction, satiety). This allows the infant to grow and explore, and eventually to become separate and autonomous.

Proximity to the attachment figure regulates emotion. Where attachment is disrupted, this can lead to permanent changes in the ability to regulate emotion.

Evidence for these propositions is apparent in the study of clinical psychiatry, most dramatically in patients who have experienced extreme disruptions of attachment e.g. where early childhood relationships have been physically, mentally or sexually abusive. Similarly if there is a history of neglect or abandonment, the subsequent development of attachment is grievously damaged.

All of these things are most characteristically observed in the study of what is known as "borderline personality disorder". Borderline personality features dramatic disturbances of affect regulation and attachment behaviour. It provides a window on processes and interactions that are universal: attachment, loss, abandonment, and rejection. In the average person these vicissitudes are more constrained and less disruptive than in those with borderline personality disorder.

Case study

Lucy was a 28-year-old woman with a diagnosis of borderline personality who lived who lived with her mother. She came for treatment because of inability to eat, feelings of depression and anxiety.

She was involved in a long-term relationship with her boyfriend James. James would frequently take off for weeks or months at a time. When he was around Lucy would spend all day and all night with James. When he was gone she would become despondent, was unable to eat and became immobilised. She had also become pregnant on three occasions and had had three therapeutic abortions.

In therapy Lucy described intense feelings of emptiness and inner longing. She felt painfully sad. She recounted that she had been given up for foster care at a very early age and recalls seeing a car carrying her mother drive away. She has felt since then an aching sense of abandonment and detachment. Ironically she had latched on to a boyfriend who repeatedly exposed her to episodes of abandonment and reunion. Her "accidental" pregnancies can be seen as an attempt to remain attached, if not to him than at least to his baby or for that matter any baby

Liat was a 20-year-old woman who had been sexually and physically abused by her father for many years, leading to a borderline personality disorder. She was referred for psychiatric help after a miscarriage. She was in an acute state of grief; she expressed the desire to die and wanted to end her life by suicide.

Her boyfriend could not leave her side and provided 24-hour care. She could not overcome the grief. Her desire to have a baby "to care for" was all consuming. She commemorated the loss of the baby by weekly prayer sessions.

Art

Themes of attachment and separation are universal within human nature and culture. These themes are reflected in art, music and cinema. Casual listening to pop music will reveal that an astonishing preponderance of popular music relates to the issues of love, attachment, separation and loss.

In art, it is hard to find anything better than the work of the Norwegian painter, Edward Munch to illustrate some of these fundamental human themes. Munch is of course universally recognized for his painting of "*The Scream*" with its haunting motifs. However, many of his other paintings are also equally expressive of the themes of loss of identity, and the pain of separation.

Munch Museum, Oslo

Figure 2. The Kiss: Edvard Munch.

In cinema it is not surprising to find that some of the most successful movies resonate with the audiences yearning for attachment and relief from separation. The movie *"Casablanca"*, often cited as the best movie ever made, is essentially a love story between Humphrey Bogart playing Rick and Ingrid Bergman playing Ilsa. There is a flashback to when the couple meet and "attach" in Paris. This is followed by an abrupt separation related to the war and then a subsequent reunion and chance encounter in Rick's bar in

Casablanca. Perhaps the movie derives its immense power from the final scene, which is a scene of separation: Rick and Ilsa are on the airport runway and the two are to be separated again, probably permanently. Surely it is this scene, more than any other, which has struck a chord with audiences over six decades of cinema history.

CHAPTER TWO

Love

Proposition #2 Strivings for attachment are the strongest
motivators of human behaviour.

Perhaps more than anything else in this world, we all long for
love: more than money, more than power, more even than sex.
But love remains difficult to define, it possesses an enigmatic
quality, beyond words, beyond rationality.

I started this discussion in chapter one with a review of attachment
and that is because attachment and love are two sides of the same
coin. Love is the subjective feeling part of attachment: the cluster of
emotions and sensations we know as love in our own experiences.

Attachment is also intimately related to separation. Separation is
the reciprocal of attachment. Similarly grief is the reciprocal of love.
In the great artistic portrayals of love, the intensity of the drama is
fuelled by the prospect and then the reality of separation and loss
e.g. Romeo and Juliet:

> "Wilt thou be gone? It is not yet near day.
> It was the nightingale, and not the lark,

> That pierced the fearful hollow of thine ear.
> Nightly she sings on yond pomegranate tree.
> Believe me love, it was the nightingale."
>
> Romeo and Juliet Act 3. Scene 5

We can feel the intense persistence of Juliet's desire to convince Romeo it is not yet morning; they both dread the separation that must come with the onset of morning, signalled by the song of the lark.

The state of "being in love" is like an obsession. The lovers cling to each other, touch each other in a re-enactment of the first attachment, the "primal love". The threat of separation causes intense anticipations of grief and pain. Separation itself leads to constant preoccupation with thoughts of the absent lover and intense yearnings for reunion. Love contains within it the seeds of future loss, the premonition of the "Sweet Sorrow" to come.

In his powerful, if pessimistic, *"Civilization and its Discontents"*, Freud observes that: "We are never so defenceless against suffering as when we love, never so forlornly unhappy as when we have lost our love object or its love." (Freud, 1930a, p. 82).

Our enduring needs for attachment and lifelong quest for love are derived from our earliest attachment relationships. Margaret Mahler, referring to the early state of mother—infant "symbiosis' says that: "The deep human connections that originate here, unlike any later connections fettered by reason and objectivity, may well be central to the deepest love, intimacy, and connection in ways that are unbounded and inarticulable" (Pine, 2004).

This early period in infant development is characterized by a lack of boundaries between mother and child; they remain psychologically merged. This reversion to a state of merger is seen in adult life as depicted in Munch's painting of *"The Kiss"* (Figure 2). Here in melancholy colouring, the figures of the man and woman embrace; the outlines of their faces blur and merge with each other.

There is a sense that our searching for attachment and love are really a search for *re-attachment,* perhaps for *reunion* with the object of our first love. There is an unconscious longing to re-find the lost primary object but simultaneously there is an unstated hope that the painful and depriving aspects of that primary love will be repaired.

Types of love

Are there different types of love? Is love for a family member, for a friend, for a spouse different in some way? And if so how? We are handicapped in the English language because we do not have the vocabulary to make these differentiations. In English we have only one word for Love; in Greek there are three: Eros, Philia and Agape. Eros refers to passionate and sexual love; Philia refers to friendship and loyalty; Agape is a love of all humanity, a transcendent love.

In the scientific literature there have been a number of classifications of different forms of love. For example there is the triangular theory of love developed by Sternberg (1986): He proposes that Love is composed of three components: Intimacy, Passion, and Commitment.

Intuitively we have a sense of what these components refer to: the warmth and non-sexual closeness of intimacy; the passion of sexual intensity and arousal; the commitment of longstanding affiliation that has been tested by the vicissitudes of life.

Sternberg (1986) says that these components may occur in varying proportions resulting in eight different types of love:

- Non-love: where all three components are absent.
- Liking: consisting of only intimacy.
- Infatuated love: consisting of passion only.
- Empty love: which is commitment only.
- Romantic love: the combination of intimacy and passion.
- Companionate love: the combination of intimacy and commitment.
- Fatuous love: which is passion and commitment.
- Consummate love: the combination of all three components.

These types may not be stable over time and there may be variations in the intensity of each component during the course of a relationship. (Hendrick C, Hendrick S, 2000). Lee (1973) distinguishes six different types of love styles:

- Romantic love (Eros) based on attractiveness, passion and sexuality.
- Game playing love which consists of "seduction, sexual freedom and sexual adventure". The avoidance of longer-term commitment.
- Best friend's love comprises mutual interests and mutual trust.

- Possessive love is an extreme version of romantic love, marked by possessiveness and jealousy.
- Pragmatic love is based on practical considerations in terms of living arrangements and particular goals such as having children.
- Altruistic love (Agape) one partner is prepared to make sacrifices for the benefit of the other and vice versa.

These categories are subsumed in two broader categories:

- Passionate love.
- Companionate love.

Passionate love consists of a state of intense longing and physiological arousal. If such love is not reciprocated there are feelings of loss, emptiness and despair.

Companionate love consists of dedication, commitment, a sense of warmth and caring and is seen as the outgrowth of long-term relationships.

Philip Roth (1994) in his novel *"The Professor of Desire"* aptly describes the shift from passionate to companionate love. The "overheated frenzy" subsides "into quiet physical affection" and:

> "We no longer *succumb* to desire, nor do we touch each other everywhere, paw and knead and handle with that unquenchable lunacy so alien to what and who we otherwise are ... now just stroking the soft long hair will do, just resting side by side in our bed each morning will do, awakening folded together, mated, in love. Yes, I am willing to settle on these terms. This will suffice." (Roth, 1994, p. 200).

Janis Abrahms Spring, a clinical psychologist in Westport Connecticut, remarks that:

> "In romantic love, your lover often becomes the single focus of your life, filling your body and soul. You have a strong desire to spend every free moment together, to merge, to become one. you think about your lover constantly ... " (Spring, 1997, p. 69).

These two types of love may have different underlying neurobiological bases (dopamine) as we shall see later. Romantic love is the love that is "blind"; that has the quality of "insanity", an obsession (Freud).

In popular songs there are frequent references to love as an addiction. There are many parallels between addiction, to powerful psychoactive drugs, and the state of being in love: a continuous longing to have more of the addicting substance, an obsessive preoccupation with the drug or object of love, feelings of elation and optimism.

It is the conventional wisdom that passionate love is not enduring and is a feature of the early months and years of a relationship. With a committed relationship, there is the continuing development and overriding of companionate love.

From an evolutionary perspective, this might reflect the need to secure a mate by a display of attractiveness and an intensity that results in sexual union and reproduction, however in the long term what is needed is security and safety that can only be provided by the development of a more mature and enduring attachment.

Case study

Nancy was a 41-year-old single woman who came into therapy sometime following her 40th birthday. This was a clichéd turning point in her life. She was troubled by the fact that she had never married and had never been able to maintain a long-term relationship. She was fraught with feelings of loneliness and foreboding about a future lived alone and the contemplation of facing advancing age and an isolated death without the support of a companion.

Not that she was not successful in engaging in romantic relationships, she was viewed as highly attractive, intelligent, outgoing and fun to be with. She had no difficulty attracting dates and courting. However, repeatedly she would find herself "falling too far, too fast" and within one or two weeks of meeting a new boyfriend, she found herself more and more preoccupied with thoughts of him when absent. She longed to hear from him by telephone or by e-mail on a daily basis. In the cases where she did not, she felt rejected, abandoned and alone with feelings of despair. Her need for constant contact for the reassurance of permanency in her relationships, paradoxically led to their premature breakup because of her intrusive possessiveness and coercive need for reassurance.

Nancy's mother had died early in her childhood. She had never felt loved by her father and grew up with a very insecure attachment.

She had a desperate longing to attach and when the opportunity arose, she became overwhelmed with fears of separation. This pattern repeated itself so often, that she was never able to maintain a long-term relationship.

The neurobiology of love

There appears to be three interconnected neural pathways that are involved in the establishment of attachment between adult pairs:

- The circuits mediating reward and re-enforcement i.e. the mesolimbic dopamine circuits.
- Circuits involving the processing of social cues which are based on neuropeptide, neurotransmission.
- Sensory information transmitted from sexual organs to the brain during sexual activity. (Young, 2005)

Romantic love is believed to be universally experienced across cultures. This has been studied using magnetic resonance imaging (Fisher H, Aron A & Brown L.L., 2005). This study showed activation in dopamine rich areas associated with reward and motivation.

Fisher and her colleagues believe that romantic love is primarily a motivation system rather than an emotion and that this drive is distinct from the sex drive. Romantic love serves the purpose of attracting mates and allows individuals to focus their energy on specific mate choices, a critical component of successful reproduction.

It is dopamine that infuses romantic love with its heightened states of tension, excitement and pleasure. It is no surprise that cocaine is among the most addictive of substances of abuse and it is cocaine that has a monstrous impact on the release of dopamine in the reward centres of the human brain.

Conversely it is the peptide oxytocin released through the hypothalamus that may form the bedrock of companionate love and long-term attachment. Oxytocin produces a feeling of connection and bonding, it is released by touching and hugging. It is released when the mother nurses her infant and in the process of parturition. Studies in prairie voles led to the theory that there is a relationship between the level of oxytocin and the proclivity to form monogamous relationships.

In the psychoanalytic view all love is transference love, an unconscious yearning for the first object of love, the mother. The experience of falling in love is triggered by the unconscious evocation of feelings reminiscent of the earliest relationship with the mother.

Michael Balint referred to this as primary object love or primary love. This is a harmonious mix of subject and object. Interestingly and paralleling the work on attachment, Balint believed that the most important senses for the mediation of love and relationships are the senses of sight and touch. For Balint "the aim of all erotic striving is to achieve the harmonious state with the object, the feeling of unity with it, as is found in primary object love" (Stuart, 2002) From this formulation it must be concluded that all love relationships are doomed to ultimately disappoint for the primary object can never be re-found.

It follows from this that all love must contain within it the seeds of disappointment: After an initial idealized and exhilarating passionate period there comes a dawning disappointment, a disillusionment because of the lack of true concordance with a primary object.

For Philip Roth the search for intimacy, as reflected in the works of Chekov, is necessary not because it brings happiness but because it is essential for survival. Yet

> "'We are born innocent ... we suffer terrible disillusionment before we can gain knowledge, and then we fear death—and we are granted only fragmentary happiness to offset the pain.' " (Roth, 1994, p. 92–94).

Disorders of love

Love has its vicissitudes and pathologies also. Salman Akhtar in "*Love and its Discontents*" (Akhtar & Kramer, 1996) describes five types of disordered love:

1. The inability to fall in love
2. The inability to remain in love
3. The tendency to fall in love with the wrong kinds of people
4. The inability to fall out of love
5. The inability to feel loved

Akhtar notes that "the cornerstone of the psychoanalytic understanding of love" (Akhtar, 1996, p. 148) was Freud's identification of two currents "whose union is necessary to ensure a completely normal attitude in love ... " (Akhtar,1996, p. 148) that is the affectionate and the sensual currents. If these currents cannot be successfully brought together, the result is a disordered expression of love. Akhtar again quotes Freud "where they love, they do not desire and where they desire, they cannot love" (Akhtar, 1996, p. 148).

The inability to fall in love is most characteristically seen in individuals with schizoid personalities. They are exquisitely fearful of closeness and remain asocial, distant, reclusive. This is obvious in their body posture; often thin and angular they sit at an undue distance; eye contact is poor; their posture is often flexed and retiring as if they are trying to make themselves invisible. In a restaurant they will sit in the remotest and most secluded corner, alone. Closeness to another gives rise to an upsurge of anxiety that threatens to overwhelm and lead to loss of cognitive focus. Unconsciously there is a terror of engulfment and loss of independent identity; a sense of psychic annihilation.

Case study

Paul was a 32-year-old single man. In early adulthood he experienced an acute psychosis, with persecutory delusions and auditory hallucinations. Over the ensuing years he was to have recurring bouts of this schizophrenic illness. He responded well to treatment with anti-psychotic medications. When well it was evident that he preferred to be alone and socialised little even when living in a group home. Listening to a Walkman was by far a safer option for him.

In interview he felt remote, distant, vacant and monotone in manner although friendly and well meaning. It was never possible for him to engage even in the most preliminary exchanges with a woman, necessary to establish a heterosexual relationship.

Others who cannot fall in love may have severe anti-social or narcissistic personalities. Both have experienced defective attachment in infancy. The anti-social personality lacks the ability to feel guilt or remorse and therefore also lacks the ability to empathise. The narcissist similarly lacks the ability to see things from the other's point of view. He cannot put himself in the other's shoes, and feel what they feel. What they love is not the other but their own projection onto the other, a projective identification.

The anti-social person views the object only in terms of its usefulness to his selfish ends. The love object is manipulated and used to meet his sexual and material needs.

There are those who have an inability to remain in love. They readily fall in love and can experience the intense romance and passion. But soon these feelings begin to wane and are replaced by an inner restlessness, a certain hankering that manifests in conflict and increasing distancing. The relationship ends and the pattern repeats itself. This may reflect a milder form of the fear experienced by the schizoid person: with intimacy comes a fear of vulnerability, the threat of losing one's identity or autonomy. This may also manifest in the repetitive "on-again-off-again" type of relationship, in men who never can commit:

Case study

Ron a 48-year-old plumber, was the peripatetic lover and friend of Doris over a period of 10 years (See chapter four). They would spend two to three months together engaging in recreational activities and sexual relations although always maintaining separate residences.

Year after year and without warning, Ron would "disappear" and be incommunicado for months at a time. This served to heighten Doris own problems with abandonment with the attendant pain of loneliness and rejection. One can only speculate (he was not a patient of mine) that Ron could not consistently maintain connection with Doris because of inner fears of engulfment. Perhaps his early attachment was infiltrated with punishment or abuse resulting in the unconscious expectation that sooner or later he was going to get hurt if he remained.

Another manifestation of this dynamic is in serial monogamy or a compulsive promiscuity. The love object is felt as an acquisition, a conquest, that once attained loses its value. What was idealized now becomes devalued and is discarded.

Akhtar's third category of disorders of love consists of falling in love with the wrong kinds of people. This pattern is well recognized by the general public and is the subject of many popular self-help

books e.g. "Ten Stupid Things Women Do To Mess Up Their Lives",
(Schlessinger 1995).

These relationships often represent re-enactments of early childhood physical or sexual abuse. This scenario may also include the
desire to rescue or save the love object; to repair psychologically the
early damaged and abusive attachment.

Case study

Donna was a 33-year-old mother of three daughters. Attractive,
auburn-haired, with an extrovert demeanor, bright, but because of
her circumstances able only to avail of a high school education. She
sought psychiatric help because of raging emotional swings: periods
of melancholy and suicidal despair interwoven with periods of elation, promiscuity and disinhibition. She was plagued by memories '
flashbacks' of early childhood sexual abuse. As a child between the
ages of six and her teenage years, she recalled trembling in her bed
at night dreading the sound of her adoptive father's steps on the
stairs, his entry to her room, to her bed and into herself. She relived
in visual and tactile memory the anguish and fear of those days and
nights; the feelings of shame, disgust, self blame and self-loathing.

Given up by her birth mother as an infant, for unknown reasons
she was adopted at three years of age. The middle-aged adoptive
parents already had two sons of their own. The little girl quickly
learned that she was privileged to have been taken in and was
given to understand that her tenure in the home was not guaran-
teed. Indeed she obviously did not naturally 'belong' there and her
impermanent status could be brought to an end at any time should
her ersatz parents so wish.

She grew up under the canopy of the twin terrors of sexual abuse
and the omnipresent threat of abandonment. The perfect formula for
the development of insecure and traumatized attachment.

In adult life this manifested as an extreme craving for a comforting
and loving relationship. She was driven by a terrible intolerance of
loneliness; every separation was felt as a cruel relived abandonment.
But often all that could be obtained was a sexual liaison. Promiscuity
represented a desperate and disappointed quest for affection. Soon
she found herself the mother of three children, each from a different
father. The promises of security and love with each male encounter

were only briefly fulfilled. Instead she was subjected to drunkenly administered physical abuse and casual infidelity.

Another subset of this group are those, often woman, who pursue only married men. This is the classic repetition of the oedipal triangle. Not only is there the unconscious longing for the father but this also may be combined with unconscious envy and competitiveness with the mother.

The inability to fall out of love is often seen in "groupies" and those unable to give up the pursuit of celebrities with whom they are infatuated. Clinically this may include the delusion that the love is reciprocated and that access to the celebrity has been thwarted by conspirators. This is known as "erotomania" and may manifest in stalking. When rebuffed there is a risk of aggression towards the object or towards the self in the form of suicide. A chilling example of this was the movie *"Notes on a Scandal"* in which the beautiful young teacher (played by Cate Blanchett) is insidiously trapped by a much older female colleague (played by Judi Dench). This movie also portrays another kind of 'wrong' love in the guise of a sexual relationship between the young teacher and a male pupil.

The inability to feel loved is equally tragic. It may be associated with deep-seated feelings of being unworthy, undeserving or defiled. The origins of this lie again in the traumatic attachment of childhood sexual abuse. Such women cannot really believe that someone could love them and may be unable to engage in the surrender of defences required for mutual consummation of love.

There are also those who are unable to feel loved because they have suppressed and repressed all feelings. Feelings are dangerous and must not be expressed. Men with severe obsessive personalities typify this form of disordered love. The affect is isolated from the thought content. Such people may seem emotionally detached, remote, cold or indifferent. There is an unreal quality to them lacking vividness and verve. They come across as wooden, monotone and flat.

Case study

Douglas was a 41-year-old dentist married for six years. He could neither feel love nor feel loved. Intellectually he could appreciate his wife loved him but he could never feel. He struggled with chronic depression and frequent thoughts of suicide. Growing up he felt his father had hated and humiliated him. He experienced murderous rage that had to be repressed and along with this all other emotions were swept out of conscious experience. His marriage was jeopardised following the birth of a baby boy, when he was unable to feel any love towards him and remained uninvolved in his care.

Monogamy and infidelity

In the movie "*The Cabin*" (Dylan Smith), three couples arrange to meet at a secluded cabin in British Columbia with the intent of exchanging sexual partners. The first couple have been in a common law relationship for many years; the second couple are married and the third, the younger couple, have just been acquainted for a matter of weeks.

The older two couples have tried to prepare themselves for the anticipated experience but very quickly things begin to unravel in a 'Pinteresque' fashion. It is apparent that exchanging sexual partners does not come without a price. This price manifests as certain associated primordial emotions that inevitably bubble to the surface: emotions of jealousy, rivalry, humiliation, debasement, and fear of loss.

This movie highlights one of the great social dilemmas in Western culture: the conflict between the desire for intense, short and passionate relationships with their associated freedom, mobility and lack of commitment versus the societal ideal of enduring monogamous relationships. Adam Phillips (1996) writes "Not every one believes in monogamy, but everyone lives as though they do." (Phillips, 1996, p. 1)

While the non-committed relationship may permit variety, exploration and adventure, there is a loss of certainty, predictability and security. On the other hand, an enduring companionate relationship may result in loss of intensity, boredom and a desire for novelty (Bauman 2003).

Adam Phillips again, has put it much more pithily: "There is always the taken-for-granted relationship and the precarious relationship, the comforting routine and the exciting risk ... we have safety and danger, habit and passion, love and lust, attachment and desire, marriage and affairs" (Phillips, 1996, p. 1).

There may be gender differences that can affect these dynamic tensions. There are some conventional although not fully substantiated proclamations that posit differences between women and men in terms of evolutionary needs. In this framework the woman is seen as desiring most of all, a stable and reliable mate who can provide security and resources. Her interest is in the long-term exclusive relationship. The goal of the male from an evolutionary point of view is to procreate with as many females as possible. It is proposed that deep in the psychological or even neurobiological core of the male, there is a proclivity for "extradyadic" relationships, something which is more commonly known as "cheating"!

"Every marriage is a disappointment" (Pittman, 1989, p. 87). Marriage can never live up to the expectations that are usually created.

Zigmunt Bauman in "Liquid Love" describes marriage as "the acceptance of the consequentiality which casual encounters refuse to accept." He states further that: "There is always a suspicion ... that one is living a lie or a mistake; that something crucially important has been overlooked, missed, neglected, left untried, and unexplored; and a vital obligation to one's own authentic self has not been met or that some chances of unknown happiness completely different from any happiness experienced before have not been taken up in time and are bound to be lost forever ... " (Bauman, 2003, p. 55).

Bauman says that in Paris, the practice of "echangisme" has become "the most popular game and the main talk of the town. This is the exchange of marital partners, more crudely known as 'wife swapping' " (Bauman, 2003, p. 52). The advantage of this pursuit is that none of the participants "is betrayed, no one's interests are threatened ... Everyone is a participant" (Bauman, 2003, p. 52).

However the film "The Cabin" puts pay to the perennial quest for utopian sexual freedom within the bounds of commitment. The tensions between exclusive attachment and the feared loss cannot be so easily dismissed by cultural arrangements.

The sex obsessed Alex Portnoy summarises the dilemma of monogamy in a pithy if perhaps crude fashion in Philip Roth's "Portnoy's Complaint": "Look, at least, I don't find myself still in my early thirties locked into a marriage with some nice person whose body has ceased to be of any genuine interest to me .... On the other hand even I must admit that there is maybe, from a certain perspective, something a little depressing about my situation, too ... the question I am willing to face is: have I anything?" (Roth, 1994, p. 102).

Perhaps like Churchill who said: "Democracy is the worst form of government, except for all those other forms that have been tried from time to time." (House of Commons speech on Nov. 11, 1947), we can say: Monogamy may be the worst form of conjugal arrangement, except for all those other forms that have been tried from time to time!

Love in cyberspace

A powerful and unforeseen onslaught on the habitual mores of western society has arisen from the widespread adoption of the Internet into our daily lives.

Email correspondence has had an astonishing effect not only on business and academic activities but also on the world of intimacy and sexuality.

What is surprising is the way this electronic and disembodied form of communication results in the incubation of intense romantic and sexual liaisons. What makes this medium, on the surface detached, linear, cognitive, so conducive to emotional intimacy?

The effect of the Internet on intimate relationships is far more seductive and alluring than for example the impact of the telephone. Why is this?

Unlike the telephone, email correspondence is more private, or at least feels so. There is time for reflection and careful construction of your message. It is also safer to say things that would be considered too risky face to face or even on the telephone, where immediate feedback might be painful or rejecting. Email allows the respondent time to reflect and carefully construct a reply. It is easier to take back or even ignore aspects of an email that may have crossed the line of comfort or appropriateness.

These are the surface features of email that provide some explanation for the torrent of intimate and sexual relationships that have developed over the past decade in "Cyberspace." But there are deeper reasons for this and to understand them we have to turn to psychoanalysis to assist us with some heuristics.

It is to Winnicott that I again turn. Winnicott, perhaps because his work is borne not only from years of careful clinical observation and scrutiny, but because he expresses his ideas with a clarity that is at once emotive and poetic. As Jacob Bronowski (1978) noted (see Introduction) a poet's ideas resonate with our own experience and this gives the poet's words a sense of universal truth.

Winnicott was most creative and original. He developed the idea of the "Transitional Object" and "Transitional Space."

Transitional space is an area between what is subjective and what is objective. Transitional space contains elements of both. It is a product of the subjective self, combined with external elements. I will return to this idea again because it contains within it the seeds of a solution to the questions I have posed in the Introduction.

Artistic work, play and fantasy are located in transitional space.

A painting contains elements from the mind of the painter: feelings, perceptions, and memories. But the painting contains more than that. It contains representations of external reality. If the painting is in the style of Realism, than the external source of the representations is easily recognized and understood. If the painting is abstract, the representations may be less clear and only understood intuitively. The artist projects parts of his inner psychic world onto the painting. The painting then is a fusion of the inner and the outer.

Perhaps Cyberspace is like painting, an area that is transitional between the subjectivity of one person and elements of another; email conveys only selective components of the writer; those the writer chooses to reveal and those that can be conveyed through the medium of electronic keyboarding.

The cell phone has also invaded our lives on a constant basis. There is now a terrible urgency for some to remain in almost constant touch. How did we ever survive the normal daily separations, the coming and goings of our lives? What is the driving compulsion to maintain telephone contact? Has our tolerance for separation been eroded by the technological possibility of continuous connection? "Stay in touch", an interesting metaphor; clearly we are not touching when we speak by phone; yet touch is one of the most powerful mediators of attachment. Is this what we are longing for, trying to obtain by pressing the cell phone to our ear to listen to the far off voice?

CHAPTER THREE

Formation of identity

Proposition #3 Identity is formed from interpersonal
interaction, and emerges from the repeated
interactions with the attachment figures.

To comprehend the shattering effect that loss has on our lives,
we must first examine the process of identity.

The idea of identity is hard to grasp and is frequently mis-
understood. Identity is often mistaken for "role". We have many
roles in our lives. A woman may be a mother, a teacher, a tennis player,
a wife, a daughter, a sister, and an artist. These roles consist of different forms of behaviour in different relationships and environments.
The concept of identity goes deeper than this. Identity is that inner
sense of who we are as persons and is made up of our inner feelings,
our view of ourselves, and our consistent responses to others. Identity is continuous over time. There are a number of interrelated terms
that may cause the reader some confusion: "identity", "personality",
"role", "ego" and "self ". In my defence I must plead that there are
no universally agreed definitions of these terms nor even a universal acceptance of their existence! I will therefore put forward some

definitions in the interests of precision and clarity. Personality is the sum of the enduring features of an individual that are observable by others. It includes habitual moods, attitudes, values and behaviours. This is what we can see from the outside: recurrent modes of relating. We can also talk about "personality disorders". These are recurrent maladaptive patterns of behaviour and relating, that cause problems for the individual or to those around him. Roles are a subset of personality and consist of those patterns that manifest in a particular context. For example a teacher will employ a role in the classroom that may be very different to his role at home as a father. In some respects we are all like the chameleon. Our roles are somewhat fluid and change in different situations; the visible parts of our personalities shift depending on the current social or interpersonal context.

"Identity" is the sense of who we are. It presupposes that humans have the faculty of apperception; we have a higher level of consciousness that can examine itself and form an inner portrayal. I use "identity" and "self" interchangeably. "Id", "Ego", and "Superego" are Freudian terms for different parts of the self. The Ego is the rational and reasonable part of the self that takes into account external reality and its demands.

There are two key elements to identity: Identity formation and identity maintenance. The American psychiatrist, Harry Stack Sullivan said that we are our experiences; it is out of our dealings with others that our sense of identity develops. In particular it is our interactions with our primary attachment figure that leads to our sense of who we are as separate and distinct persons. It is the loving responses of the mother that gives us good feelings about ourselves. As the old saying goes "you're nobody till somebody loves you"!

At birth, the infant does not have sufficient cognitive functioning to be conscious of the fact that he or she is a separate individual. In the earliest weeks of life, the infant is unable to differentiate between what comes from inside itself and what comes from outside itself. In other words, the infant cannot distinguish what is "me" and what is "not-me".

Margaret Mahler theorises that the infant and mother are in a psychological symbiotic state. In her terminology, this is the "autistic" phase of development. The infant feels inner disturbances, pain, hunger, cold and cries out. The mother responds with food, warmth, and contact. The infant is not aware of where its inner needs end and the response of the mother begins. However, the mother is not always there to respond and the infant perceives that there is something separate from himself and begins to develop an inner model of what is internal and what is external.

Environments vary greatly in quality. Caregivers vary greatly in what they can and are able to give. The material circumstances of each child vary greatly and there may be deprivation of essential nutrients and essential care.

No maternal response can be perfect. It is important that the baby's principal needs for nurturance, affection and care are met but they cannot be met 100% of the time. There is gratification of needs but also some deprivation. It is the balance of these two poles that makes up the quality of the maternal environment. Winnicott formulated the idea of "good enough mothering". There is a requisite level of responsiveness if the infant is to develop in a healthy way and eventually to experience good mental health.

I am using the term maternal environment not just to refer to the quality of the relationship between the mother and the baby but in general to the care giving environment that may include mother, father, other relatives, who participate in responding to the infant's needs and in conveying love and affection to him. There is usually one particular person that has primary responsibility for this and so the other caregivers are referred to as "secondary" attachment figures.

For the maternal environment to be successful, it is necessary that the basic physical and material needs of the family are met. There must be adequate shelter, food, and protection from danger. Additionally, the family environment must be such that the mother has the emotional resources and equanimity to respond to her infant child. When the infant's needs for food and comfort are met, the infant feels a sense of fulfilment and satisfaction. As such interactions are repeated over time, the infant is able to develop an inner sense of peace and security which Erikson (1950) called "basic trust". In Bowlby's terms, we would call this a sense of secure attachment and an awareness of a secure base.

Conversely, if the infant's needs are not met on a timely basis the inner feelings of hunger and discomfort are repeatedly experienced giving rise to a deficient inner sense of trust, security and peace.

The part of the mother that is able to respond to the infant's needs is experienced as "the good mother" in Melanie Klein's terminology. The part of the mother that is not responsive is felt as the depriving "bad mother". The good mother is associated with states of satiety and comfort. In other words, there is an inner state that matches the external response and the "the good mother" becomes associated with good inner feelings. In the language of object relations theory, the good object becomes internalized.

In a similar fashion, the bad mother becomes associated with the unpleasant, bad internal feelings: a bad object is internalized. In this way the foundation of each infant's identity is laid down and these internalized representations form the basic building blocks for all that is to come.

In an environment where there is marked deprivation, neglect, and physical or sexual abuse, the internalizations will be correspondingly vicious, harsh and tormenting. The infant's sense of self will follow this pattern.

Needless to say, the foundation stone that is laid down in the first two to three years of life will have a critical impact on all experiences that are to follow in the course of development. This is true not only psychologically but also biologically. The nature of the maternal environment directly affects the developing brain. The growth of neurons and the development of neurocircuits are strongly influenced by the quality of the attachment between mother and child. The sum total of internalized objects and their corresponding connections to the self make up the identity of the individual. A preponderance of the bad experiences, of unmet needs leads to a preponderance of negative feelings and views of one's self.

The bedrock of identity formation is laid down in the early months and continues into in the first three years of life. This coincides with rapid developments in the brain. If the early environment is responsive and nurturing a sense of inner security is established. This is accompanied by a positive disposition towards the external world. If the early environment is harsh and disappointing the infant develops with a sense of insecurity and a foreboding outlook on life. This does not mean that subsequent experience will not have an impact on identity formation. The influence of the father, siblings, extended family, kindergarten, school and peers are all-important. However the early foundational basis formed in the first three years will influence all subsequent development. The early dynamic of attachment will form a central thread in all subsequent development like a leitmotiv in a symphony. The brain will never again be so "plastic" or vulnerable to outside influence.

The adolescent years represent a second critical period of identity formation. Propelled by physical and intellectual changes and social demands this is a time when significant shaping takes place. The upsurge of sexual drives and the distancing from the parental sources of attachment lead the adolescent to explore intimate relationships. This is a peak time for dating and falling in love. The teen is learning to become less dependent on parents. Attitudes, beliefs, values and behaviour are influenced more by peers. Parental values and norms are challenged. The adolescents self-view goes through a process of transition and reconfiguration. But the earlier themes pervade and inform these subsequent developmental stages.

There is another important foundation stone that I have not yet discussed. This derives from genetic factors which endow each infant with inherited temperaments. Mothers often remark that each of their babies was different right from the time of birth. Babies differ in sleep-wakefulness patterns, level of activity, character of mood, attention span and distractibility. These differences will evoke different qualities of response in the caregivers. For example a baby that wakes often in the night and is irritable may receive a more harried and fatigued response from its mother than his long sleeping and relaxed sister!

Cloninger (in Svrakic 2002) has identified four temperamental traits that are present from the time of birth: novelty seeking, harm avoidance, reward dependence and persistence. Temperaments are neurobiological dispositions and predate the effect of attachment. They are the raw "stuff" out of which emotions will be shaped in response to the environment. This is why individuals raised in the same environment may turn out to have very different personalities. The attachment relationship does not operate on a "tabula rasa" (a blank slate). Temperament and maternal response interact in an iterative process throughout development.

Harm avoidance is characterized by worry, pessimism, fear of uncertainty, shyness and fatigability. Novelty seeking consists of exploratory behaviour, impulsiveness and extravagance. Reward dependence includes sentimentality, openness to communication and dependence. The temperament of persistence is associated with industriousness, enthusiasm and perfectionism. Thus we can construct an equation for the formation of the sense of identity and personality:

> Inborn temperament + quality of attachment relationships + later life experiences = basis of personality and sense of identity.

It is crucial to note that we cannot give free expression to our innermost feelings and impulses at all times. The gratification of our needs for love, sexual relations, and aggressive urges have to be constrained by the demands of civilized society. Certain aspects of our selves can only be revealed in special circumstances, usually in special relationships.

The mechanisms that we automatically use to prevent the unfettered expression of our inner selves are known as "defence mechanisms". A defence mechanism is a psychological operation that is automatically and unconsciously deployed when an individual is facing a psychological threat. Defences protect the person by keeping certain thoughts and feelings out of awareness. In Freudian conflict theory the threat is conceptualized as arising from internal drives and impulses (aggressive, sexual) that threaten the ego resulting in anxiety.

In object relations theory the threat arises out of relationships. Defences serve to keep the undesirable feelings related to self or object representations out of awareness. Threats may be to self-esteem; to the ego; to bodily integrity; to self-image. Threats may come from external events, dangers or losses.

Defensive patterns manifest in all our relationships. Common defence mechanisms include: repression which keeps threatening ideas, impulses and feelings out of awareness; denial refers to a similar process that blocks out aspects of external reality. Sublimation is channelling unacceptable feelings or impulses into socially acceptable behaviour. Reaction formation is converting an unacceptable wish or impulse into its opposite. For example unconscious feelings of hostility are converted into an overly nice and solicitous demeanour. Intellectualization is the avoidance of feelings by focusing on abstract ideas, stripped of emotion. Projection is a psychological operation by means of which unacceptable, threatening feelings, wishes or impulses are expelled from the subject and attributed to another person. Identification is where the subject takes on aspects of the other person's behaviours, attributes or feelings as part of himself.

We modify our wishes, feelings and impulses by means of repression, sublimation, intellectualization, projection, reaction formation, and other defence mechanisms. Particularly if we grow up in a hostile environment that is belittling, abusive or rejecting we may have to repress and suppress the spontaneous expression of our true selves. We may then develop unconsciously a set of surface behaviours and defences that disguise our true self. This is what Winnicott described as the "false self".

The "false self" consists of a constellation of defences that mask the expression of the true inner self. This arises when the environment is not "good enough" and prevents the development of the individual's innate potential. The true self is obscured. In a frustrating and non-loving environment a false self emerges by repressing the true impulses and replacing these by conformity to the hostile demands of the parental environment. The false self ensures psychological survival by "not making waves"; the false self lacks the vitality and unfettered spontaneity of the true self.

The As-If personality

A similar idea was put forth by the psychoanalyst Helene Deutsch. In an intriguing paper published in the Psychoanalytic Quarterly in 1942, Deutsch described individuals who on the surface appeared engaging, bright even gifted but who lacked in their relationships any sense of warmth. Emotional expression was stilted and lacking in vigour:

> "It is like the performance of an actor who is technically well trained but who lacks the necessary spark to make his impersonations true to life."

Such individuals manifest an intangible lack of genuineness. They have "a highly plastic readiness" and like chameleons automatically identify with what others are feeling and thinking. Instinctual drives are suppressed. Anger or aggression may be replaced by compliance and obedience. Affect is restricted and constrained, lacking warmth and spontaneity.

Persons with As-If personalities may attach themselves to religious or political groups so as to fill their inner emptiness by identification with the group norms and beliefs. They are easy prey for totalitarian movements that hold out the false promise of certainty and direction. These and similar personalities submit to the will and commands of the omnipotent political leader.

Case study

Virginia was a 46-year-old director of a large social service agency. Highly regarded for her competence by her colleagues she nevertheless felt she was a "fraud". Her relationships were marked by an unrelenting need to please and to conform to the wishes of others. Her own wishes and instincts were suppressed, and she displayed a neutral, pleasing but lukewarm affect. Because any spontaneous affect had to kept under such tight control her subjective feelings were sterile, empty and hollow.

Therapy focused on helping her become aware of her suppressed longings and emotions and challenging her defensive people pleasing. She subsequently broke out of a constraining marital relationship by having an extramarital affair. This may have represented a more valid expression of her inner core.

Case study

Penelope was a 36-year-old unmarried surgeon who presented with symptoms of depression and anxiety following the death of her 68-year-old mother. She was recognized for her high level of competence and good looks. Her patients were always happy with the care she delivered. It was surprising then when she revealed in therapy that she felt undeserving of love. In her relationships with men she always held back and could not give herself completely. Inwardly she felt she was not a good person despite all the praise and admiration she received from her patients and colleagues. Her mother had been verbally abusive and favoured her sister. Penelope was put down and undermined.

Because of her inner sense of badness she dedicated her life to helping others at the expense of her own needs and desires. Her true feelings were suppressed and repressed. Her sense of self developed in order to comply with external demands that are by trying to anticipate her mother's needs and attempting to please her. In other words she evolved a "false self".

In therapy the focus was on helping her to identify her true underlying feelings and wishes. As a result she became more spontaneous and open in her relationships and eventually was able to achieve a fulfilling marriage.

This chapter establishes proposition #6: that a major aspect of identity formation arises out of the dyadic attachment relationship: Inborn temperament combined with the quality of attachment relationships and later life experiences are the basis of personality and the sense of identity. Where there is a "good enough" environment a secure sense of self develops. This allows for mutually satisfying relationships unhampered by overly restrictive defences.

CHAPTER FOUR

Emotions and moods

Proposition # 4a Mood is the bedrock of identity and sense
of self
Proposition # 4b Instability of mood gives rise to instability
of the sense of identity

Mood is emotion sustained over a period of time. To appreciate the role of mood in love and loss, I will first review the nature and function of the key emotions.

In addition to love, a series of other emotions play a dominant role in our everyday lives, the emotions of anger, fear, joy, sadness and playfulness. These emotions are universal throughout human society and are evident in our mammalian ancestors. But just what is an emotion? When we feel fear or anger, just what are we in fact feeling? What is the source of such feelings?

The human brain has evolved from its animal precursors over millions of years. Broadly we can view the brain as having a three-part structure (Maclean, 1973): 1) the Reptilian brain, which we share with our reptile ancestors; 2) the Paleomammalian and 3) the Neomammalian brain. The Neomamalian brain includes the vast human neocortex which gives humans advanced intellectual and language abilities.

Our emotions arise from the older Reptilian and Paleommalian regions. These regions constitute the Limbic System (Papez), which is largely located below the cortex.

Several core emotional systems have been identified in mammals (Panksepp, 1998), which are linked to social bonding, separation distress, sexuality, anger, fear and joy. Emotions can be regarded as feeling–action systems. They are programmed responses to distinct stimuli that result in both subjective feelings as well as physiological and action responses. We are most familiar with the subjective feeling part of emotion, what we experience and express through speech, facial expression, posture, and gesture. Each emotion is also accompanied by physiological and bodily changes that prepare the body for the potential action which may be required. For example, an external threat of physical harm will induce the emotion of fear; this includes physiological changes such as increased heart rate, increased respirations, heightened vigilance and a readiness for the complex actions of fighting or fleeing.

It is evident that these action programs serve a critical survival function for the animal. Such action programs operate very quickly and do not have to go through the slower cognitive processes of the higher brain. In summary we can say that:

Emotion = subjective feeling + physiological changes + action

Emotional systems can be compared to computer operating systems. This depends firstly on the "hardware", the brain, its neurons, its nuclei and circuits; as well as the "software" which consist of genetically programmed series of operations, actions and communication.

There has long been a debate as to which is primary in the generation of emotions: is it the bodily and physiological changes that give rise to the subjective feelings and sensations that we know as emotion or, is it the triggering of the feeling state that gives rise to the bodily changes? The debate is not completely resolved but it seems most likely that emotions are triggered by some external cues that activate the emotion-action program.

In the discussion of attachment in chapter one, it was proposed that there is a specific neural circuit that is the basis for the feelings and behaviours connected to attachment. Panksepp has proposed that there are specific neural circuits that underlie each of the primary emotions.

The following are the key primary emotion action programs as described by Panksepp (2004).

- The attachment system, which includes social bonding and separation distress. Specific areas of the brain involved are outlined Panksepp and these circuits are active in both the infant and the parent. When activated, the infant seeks the attachment figure for care and protection. The corresponding neural circuits are activated in the parent/attachment figure to respond appropriately and reinforce the attachment bond. The peptide hormone oxytocin plays a critical role within these neural circuits.
- Sexuality, mating and reproduction are served by another set of circuits, which are separate from, although with some overlap to the attachment circuits. Oxytocin and opioids have important roles in both sets of circuits. I want to stress the point that the attachment circuit and the sexual circuit although overlapping are separate and this provides some perspective on the age old social conflict as to whether sex can be separated from love in our relationships.

There are differences in the neurobiology of female and male sexuality with oxytocin, playing the leading role in females. Vasopressin neurons are the basis for male sexuality. Oxytocin and opioids are involved in orgasm within both sexes. Oxytocin activity in the brain is facilitated by estrogen and progesterone. Vasopressin is linked to the male hormone testosterone.

- The emotion of anger and its associated system is based in a neural circuit that begins in the medial amygdala. This system is triggered by external threat or frustration of goals.
- The emotion of fear is activated again in response to threat. This may trigger a fighting or fleeing action response.

Fear consists of the subjective feeling of apprehension that manifests in higher cognitive functioning as worrying and an attempt to appraise the nature of the threat. There is associated autonomic arousal with increased heart rate, respirations and shifts of blood flow within the body. The action response or motor behaviour may consist of freezing, fighting or fleeing. Particular postures, facial expressions and gestures are also part of the operating program and serve a communicative function to others.

- The emotion of joy, according to Panksepp, is related to a "rough and tumble play—joy system" again located in the sub cortical areas of the brain in mammals. Activation of this circuit leads to feelings of joy and exhilaration. Rough and tumble play may represent a rehearsal behaviour in young animals, which in adult life may manifest in forms of social competition and domination. Physical contact, "tickle skin" and laughter are components of this circuit (Panksepp, 2004, p. 57).

In human evolution, a number of secondary or complex emotions have evolved as a result of linkages with specific cognitive and social situations, i.e. the emotions of shame, guilt, jealousy, envy, embarrassment and pride. These may be derivatives of the primary emotions that have evolved in response to social and interpersonal threats rather than threats of bodily harm or death.

The emotions of envy and jealousy are important in any consideration of love and loss. Jealously is a compound emotion involving love, the threat of loss, and hatred. It is based in a three-way relationship: the subject, the love object and the rival. It consists of feelings of love and fear of loss towards the love object; feelings of hatred towards the rival and the betraying lover. Jealousy is about possession of the love object and the threat of losing it. The love object is exalted but at the same time denigrated. Hate and love become mixed in ambivalence.

Envy surprisingly is quite different. Within the Kleinian School of Psychoanalysis envy is regarded as a primary innate emotion. Envy involves two not three people. The subject feels deprived; a feeling of "not having". "Others have, I have not!" There is a feeling of being excluded, of being robbed. Envy comprises a desire to destroy and it is this component that lends it an importance in the quest for the meaning of life. For this reason we will return to it in the section on Eros and Thanatos.

While some of the most basic processes of these operating systems arise in the most primitive areas of our brains, the "Reptilian" brain, the more social-promoting emotions and operating systems arise from the mammalian layers of the brain. The development of the neocortex in humans adds another layer to the experience of emotions in the form of symbolic and linguistic representations and the ability to override the emotional expression in the lower areas of the brain. Indeed this is the basis for cognitive behavioural therapy. This is an attempt to superimpose the rational reasoning brain on the more primitive emotional brain. In Freudian language it is the attempt of the Ego to deal with the Id.

Cognitive behavioural therapy, (CBT), is focused on the higher levels of the brain, on specific cognitions that influence underlying feeling states. In cognitive theory it is believed that specific thoughts, "distorted thoughts" can influence the feeling part of emotion. For example, the thought that "I am a failure" will give rise to feelings of depression. By attempting to replace these thoughts by thoughts that are more objectively based on reality, the goal is to overcome the sub-cortical feelings of depression. However, a converse view is that the cognitions are secondary to the underlying emotion, that is, that the emotion of depression is primary at a sub-cortical level and gives rise to corresponding cognitions of failure and unworthiness. In psychiatry medications work at these sub-cortical levels to alter the neurochemistry that underlies the feeling parts of emotion. Psychodynamic psychotherapy focuses very strongly on the identification and expression of underlying emotions (sub-cortical) and the contradictions, conflicts, social and personal meaning of these feeling states in the individual's life.

In line with the thesis of this book that it is love and loss that are central to the human condition, I would like to emphasize that the neural circuits underlying sexuality, fear and rage are embedded in the survival needs of the organism. It is also true that the attachment circuit promotes the survival of the infant by ensuring that it remains in proximity to a protective and caring adult. The caring adult, the maternal attachment figure also has within her a reciprocal neural circuit that underlies maternal and caring behaviours. It is my contention that it is the attachment circuit that is related to our quest for meaning in life and holds the prospect for the discovery of our true essential nature: our core self.

All of these emotional circuits may be linked in some ways to the reward motivating system of the brain. This is located in the areas known as the ventral segmental area and the nucleus accumbens. The functions of this system are mediated by the neurotransmitter Dopamine. The release of Dopamine in these areas of the brain gives rise to feelings of joy, meaningfulness and exhilaration. All drugs of abuse stimulate this system, most dramatically cocaine, which most powerfully stimulates the release of Dopamine. Unfortunately, over time the Dopamine receptors become less and less responsive requiring higher and higher doses of the drug (tolerance). The drug-induced state is followed by a crash, a precipitous drop in the euphoria to a state of unmitigated depression. Thus, substances of abuse such as cocaine, amphetamines, and heroin have not lived up to the hippie promise of human happiness. On the contrary, they represent a Faustian bargain that ultimately ends in the enslavement of the human soul and self-destruction.

The most primitive emotional systems of fear and aggression are critical to the individual's and group survival. Throughout our animal and human evolutionary past, it is these emotions that have played the most powerful role in the survival of the fittest. From ancient times, animals and man have been involved in wars of aggression for the control of food, resources and territory. Indeed the biological urges related to hunting, inter-male and interspecies aggression have dominated human history up until the dawn of civilization and beyond.

The evolution of the higher brain functions has been associated with an attempt to override these primitive aggressive instincts and replace them by civil society based on a respect for human life. Clearly we have largely failed in this endeavour as war, human conflict, murder and exploitation remain prevalent throughout the world. These neural circuits remain linked to the ventral segmental reward system so that unfortunately there is a certain pleasure and positive emotional valence attached to the exercise of aggression (see section on perversions). Forces of cruelty and sadism are no less present in our own day than they were among our primitive ancestors 10,000 years ago.

We will not find human salvation in these reptilian neural circuits. Perhaps our salvation can be found in the socially promoting mammalian attachment based neurobiology, that is the neural circuits that underlie our subjective feelings of love, caring and compassion. Maybe the potential saving grace for the human species is "make love not war". This may be now as profound as it is trite but nevertheless, remains true. Our primitive reptilian and old mammalian instincts of aggression, rage and warfare are now accompanied by

21st century technology wherein weapons of mass and catastrophic destruction can be wielded by small bands of instinctively driven groups of men.

The battle continues between good and evil, creation and destruction, love and death, Eros and Thanatos.

Moods

We all live with variations of mood on a constant day to day basis but it is remarkably difficult for us to appreciate the fundamental nature of mood states. Even more mysteriously, it may not be apparent that mood is intimately related to attachment, love, and loss. Additionally, it may be surprising to the reader that mood is a fundamental building block of the sense of human identity.

Mood is sustained emotion. Mood may be regarded as analogous to climate. It is the background, the context, the ambiance, that provides for the normal functioning of the human animal. It is the stable and normative balance of mood that allows for optimal physical and mental functioning; a state known as "euthymia". I am particularly interested in two key moods that form the ambience that underlies our day-to-day functioning: joy and sadness.

In medicine there is a long tradition of learning about normal body processes from the study of disease. In neurology much has been learned about the normal functioning of the brain by studying individuals who suffer from brain trauma or brain diseases such as stroke, by correlating loss of functions with the areas of the brain that had been damaged by the disease. For example loss of speech after stroke was found to be the result of damage to Broca's area of the brain. Similarly in our present exploration we can learn about normal emotional functioning and normative moods by studying people who are prone to pathologically extreme variations of mood and emotion.

There are two sources. Firstly, our earlier account of attachment and attachment behaviour demonstrated that the infant's affective state was regulated by the degree of proximity to the secure base, the object of attachment.

Secondly, we can learn about the function and importance of mood by studying instances where things go wrong, where mood is disordered.

Among the derangements of mood that form a central preoccupation of psychiatrists in their daily work are:

- Depression.
- Bipolar mood disorder consisting of depression and mood elevation.
- Borderline personality disorder comprising centrally a disorder of mood regulation.

A person with borderline personality disorder exhibits profound dysregulation of mood and emotion. This results from the combination of inherited temperament and abnormal attachment experiences (Eppel, 2005). The impact of this dysregulation is profound, affecting behaviour, relationships, ability to function at work or school, and ultimately leading to urges towards self-destruction.

The instability of mood provokes an exquisite sensitivity to rejection by others and an all-engulfing desire to merge or fuse with a love object. Put in terms of attachment theory, there is a compelling preoccupation with the need to be in proximity to an attachment figure that can provide safety and a secure base. When inevitably such a tall order cannot be met, the individual experiences profound despair, depression, loss and abandonment that ultimately may lead to an attempt at suicide. So without love, without attachment, there is no life worth living.

From this we can infer that loss, the subjective feelings and mood state that accompany loss, abandonment or rejection are the reciprocal of those feelings that are found in the state of being in love or being securely attached. Severe depression is accompanied by feelings of profound aloneness, emptiness and meaninglessness.

Case study

Doris was a 53-year-old divorced woman, mother of two children, her son Tom, 26, and a daughter Sophie, age 24. She had grown up in a large family with three brothers and three sisters. Life was chaotic in the home and the family struggled financially. Doris described her father as caring but largely absent due to his need to hold down two jobs to support the large family. Doris described her mother as warm, but recalls feeling that her mother had little time for her due to the demands of her siblings. Doris did well at school and completed some college courses. After this she obtained a good secretarial position in a moderate sized company and was praised for her efficiency and accuracy. She was outgoing, friendly and had a good sense of humour. She dated normally and married in her mid 20s and had the two children with her first husband. The marriage lasted 12 years and ended after her husband had an extramarital relationship. The second marriage was characterized by a lot of conflict and strife and ended after two years.

Doris struggled to bring up her children. Tragically in her mid 30s she began to experience periods of depression requiring psychiatric treatment. One spring she began to experience abnormally increased energy, felt that her body was speeded up and she could not sleep despite feeling tired and exhausted by the urge to be constantly moving. Her mood alternated between periods of elation and irritability and she became angry and argumentative in public. She had to be taken to the hospital by the police and was admitted for several weeks and given the diagnosis of bipolar disorder. She was treated with mood stabilizers and antidepressants but continued to undergo repeated bouts of depression and mania. She also experienced mixed states, a combination of depressed mood, agitation, irritability and increased levels of suicidal thoughts. At one point, she took a large overdose of medications and required care in the ICU at a local teaching hospital.

Throughout the ravages of a severe form of this disease, in fact a rapid cycling variant, she did the best she could in raising her children and providing them with affection and care. This was made more difficult by the constant battle with poverty, inability to work and the limits of disability payments. The children were exposed to repeated separations when Doris became ill and required periods of hospitalization.

Doris has been aware since her childhood that she found being alone difficult. She became very depressed following the end of her marriages and often felt abandoned and alone. She found some solace in caring for her two children, but as they grew became more reliant on them to meet her own needs for affection and support. Tom moved out when he was about eighteen years of age and found a job in a nearby city. Sophie stayed home with her mother. Doris has found it difficult to see her son move out and move to another town and experienced much sadness and anxiety in response to this separation. She became more dependent on Sophie. Sophie was very attentive and caring and when Doris became depressed, Sophie stayed home to support her and provided words of solace and comfort. However, as Sophie reached her late teens she started developing her own life and began to stay out late at night, visiting friends and dating, Doris found this very difficult. She felt deserted and abandoned by Sophie despite her years of support and attentiveness to her mother. It was at this point that Doris came under my care for the treatment of her illness.

Treatment consisted initially of attempting to stabilize Doris' bipolar illness by treatment with mood stabilizers. Antidepressants were discontinued because of the possibility of worsening the long-term course of the illness by means of accelerating the cycles of depression and mania. Secondly, psychotherapy was undertaken and it became apparent early on that the theme of abandonment and separation was central in Doris' life. Not only had she experienced major losses and separations in terms of her marriages, but continued to struggle with smaller day-to-day separations such as the departure of her children even when temporary. She found it particularly difficult when Sophie stayed over night with friends and Doris would feel very abandoned and angry that she had been left alone. At times these feelings of abandonment and rejection reached the point where she felt that there was no longer any reason to live and she contemplated suicide.

These feelings were complicated by the fact that she had struck up a relationship with a single man of similar age. At the time of starting therapy with me, Doris had been involved with this man for several years. However, the relationship was very disconnected. For months at a time she would see her boyfriend, Ron (See chapter 2), almost on a daily basis and they were sexually active together. However, without warning, Ron would leave and there would be no contact between them for weeks or months. The relationship was one of constant oscillation of returns and departures. With each departure, Doris struggled with increasing levels of abandonment and loneliness, again often leading to thoughts of suicide.

The focus of therapy was to help her understand her sensitivity to abandonment and relating her feelings towards her children to the feelings that she had experienced in her past relationships and as a child during her development. Typically her feelings of abandonment surfaced within the therapy relationship when even after developing a solid therapeutic alliance with the therapist over two years, she continued to experience times of the therapist's vacation as evidence of abandonment of her. With time she gained more understanding and insight to these feelings and increased her tolerance for separation and was able to allow her children to develop increased levels of independence and autonomy.

The individual with bipolar disorder experiences states of mood elevation, which are exhilarating and extremely pleasurable. They are associated with a sense of enhanced abilities, physical vigour and mental functioning. There is a sense of inflation, over-confidence and increased sexual drive. These features resemble in many ways the experience of romantic love and may derive from underlying peregrinations of the Dopamine neurotransmitter!

People with borderline personality are described as lacking a stable sense of personal identity. Compare this with individual who has rapid cycling or even ultra-rapid cycling bipolar mood disorder. One week, such an individual feels in the depths of despair, his world outlook is pessimistic and gloomy; he has no sense of personal energy, vigour, ambition or motivation. The following week, he may experience a surge of mania with an inflation of energy, ambition, sex drive, the desire to interact socially and to engage on new projects. From one week to the other, his central core, his self perception, is changed dramatically by the underlying shift in mood.

It is from such experiences that we learn that the sense of self and sense of identity, is very much dependent on the background mood state, upon the ambient "climate" within which cognitive and physical functioning takes place.

The absence of a stable mood system thus has very far-reaching effects. The loss of a continuous sense of self, a continuous sense of identity, leads to confusion as to goals, ambition and abilities. What is desired and what is desirable cannot be properly evaluated because these attributes change when the mood climate changes. Relationships are subject to the dramatic shifts of mood and viewpoints, are constructed under the impact of depression and elation.

Case study

Karen was a 38-year-old married mother of two. She has suffered for 15 years with ultra-rapid cycling bipolar II mood disorder. This consists of days of deep suicidal black depression followed by an elevated mood; increased energy, gregariousness and creative productiveness. When depressed her energy interest and motivation are low. Her view of the world is pessimistic; her view of her self is coloured by guilt, shame and feelings of inadequacy. When her mood is elevated she is confident, outgoing, ambitious, optimistic and productive. These states switch so rapidly that she is confused as to which reflects her "true" self: the pessimistic or the optimistic. There is no sense of a continuous self because of the rapid fluctuations of mood.

Art and emotion

Art reveals much of our inner life, the truth about human nature; but what is art and why does it resonate so much with us? Art is a transitional space where the inner joins with the outer (Winnicott), "a halfway house between subjective and objective" (Laplanche & Pontalis 1973, p. 465). It is the place where elements of the inner emotional life combine with elements of the external world to form a concrete portrayal that can be visually and or auditorily perceived, e.g. painting, architecture, sculpture, cinema (visual) or music, poetry (auditory).

By studying the artist's work we can come to understand parts of the artist's inner emotional world. More correctly we resonate with those parts of his inner life that strike a cord with us, because they constitute elements which are universal in human nature.

Nowhere is this more vividly and even frighteningly expressed than in the paintings of Edvard Munch. "The Scream" is amongst his best-known works and formed for many years a staple illustration of psychiatric torment. The lower dark portion of The Scream portrays a sense of profound blackness and associated existential terror. The redness in the sky above portrays the ferocious agitation associated with mania.

Munch has painted many other paintings depicting the blackness of depression and the grief of loss and separation for example, "The Sick Child", "Evening on Karl Johan Street", "Anxiety", and "The Lonely Ones". These can be viewed online at various museum sites (e.g. the Munch Museum in Oslo).

"The Sick Child" portrays Munch's sister when she was gravely ill. The child is propped up in bed; beside her an older woman dressed in black, with head deeply bowed in an expression of grief, grasps her hand. The scene evokes great sadness and conveys a sinister sense of impending death.

"Evening on Karl Johann Street" is ghoulish and uncanny. Dark black infuses violets and grey conjuring up an emotion of oppressive bleakness.

"Anxiety" echoes *"The Scream"*, with dark, black figures in the foreground while above the sky is a violent red. Like *"The Scream"* this is a mixture of profound depression and manic agitation. It might well be a depiction of a mixed mood state. Such moods are a feature of Bipolar disorder and are experienced as horrific and which are often accompanied by urges to suicide.

In *"The Lonely Ones"* a girl in white and a man in black are standing on the seashore. We see them from behind; we cannot see their faces. The couple are set apart and seem unaware of each other's presence. The effect is one of sadness and aloneness.

It is through such paintings that emotions and mood can be objectified and literally visualised so that we can comprehend them in deeply resonant ways.

Music and emotion

The meaning of music is an enigma. Music is a prominent part of our affairs. We listen to it on the car radio, and we go to dances. Music is played at public ceremonies, celebrations of weddings and every special occasion. Music accompanies motion pictures.

It is intriguing to consider how little we really understand about the role and meaning of music. We all take it for granted and as such it is something unquestioned. Yet, why should rhythmic sounds affect us? At first glance it seems to have something to do with emotions. Music evokes emotions. It also evokes rhythmic body movement, known as "dance". Feelings plus action is a pattern we have come to recognize in the key emotions identified above.

One has to recall that our human and animal ancestors did not have language. Earliest human speech consisted of sounds. The sounds could be varied in length, amplitude, pitch, and rhythm. Infants at birth when faced with separation from the attachment figure emit vocalizations called sounds that we refer to as "crying". A mother learns quickly to distinguish the different sounds made by her baby: the sounds of distress which rise and fall rhythmically;

the sounds of murmured satisfaction and contentment; the sharp sounds and response to fear or alarm; the sounds associated with hunger or pain. The recognition of these sounds is very important in the mother infant relationship. Could it be that when we listen to sad themes of separation and loss that we are hearing echoes and elaborations of those early separation vocalizations? The melancholy appeal of the blues must derive from its ability to tap into the emotional source of sadness in our brains.

Music evokes and communicates emotion. It is the language of emotion which is far more powerful than the verbal language of our neocortex. Music is the language of those areas of the brain that form the neural circuits of emotion: it is the language of the limbic system.

One can go further and say that some music represents the metre and rhythm of more primitive bodily functions. Does the beating of drums represent the beating of the mother's heart as the baby lies against her breast? Does the sound of drums evoke in us some unconscious memories of our earliest experiences? Are the rhythms of sexual interplay paralleled in the movements of dance? Do some of the sounds replicate the mating calls of our animal ancestors?

At the very least, we can say that the impact of music is powerful and deep. It affects us at our deepest emotional levels. It is enlisted to rally the troops before battle and to stir the congregants in prayer. Likewise poetry derives its emotive power because of its rhythmic and metrical properties.

It is often through song and melody it is often through song and melody that our most powerful emotions are given expression. The fact that the overwhelming preponderance of popular music revolves around feelings of love and loss illustrates the centrality of these emotional themes throughout our lives.

Again it is to Panksepp (2002) that I must attribute the origin and formulation of these ideas. In describing the type of music that can cause us to experience a "chill" or "send shivers" down the spine they write that:

> "… a high pitched sustained crescendo, a sustained note of grief sung by a soprano or played on a violin (capable of piercing the 'soul' so to speak) seems to be an idea stimulus for evoking chills. A solo instrument, like a trumpet or cello … is especially evocative" (Panksepp & Bernatzky, 2002).

The authors go on to say that these feelings are provoked by "sad music that contains acoustic properties similar to the separation call of young animals, the primal cry of despair ..."

These separation vocalizations have the purpose of signalling to the attachment figure the need for proximity, care and attention.

Reciprocally, music may have the property of regulating and quieting distressed moods by replicating some of the emotions felt in the context of proximity and maternal care.

CHAPTER FIVE

Psychiatric disorders and love and loss

Proposition #5 Psychiatric disorders both reflect and effect the expression of love and loss.

Personality types

The meaning and significance of the concept of "personality", as we saw in chapter three, has been the subject of debate for many decades. Within psychiatry two types of personalities are broadly recognized, those that are deemed normal and those that are deemed abnormal. Personality refers to enduring traits and characteristics of an individual that persist throughout his life and are formed early in development.

Personality type is determined by a combination of inborn temperaments, the quality of attachment relationships and later life events. Each personality type is distinguished by an associated combination of defence mechanisms. For example obsessive personality is associated with the defences of intellectualization and reaction formation; projection is one of the defences routinely seen in people with borderline personality.

Many of the personality disorders are commonly recognized within our culture and vernacular. We have all heard of narcissistic, obsessive, histrionic and dependent personality types. In the official classification of the American Psychiatric Association, the Diagnostic and Statistical Manual (DSM) 4th edition, each personality disorder has a list of criteria which must be fulfilled in order for a diagnosis to be made. This classification gives the mistaken impression that personality types are in fact unique categories. In reality, nobody is a pure narcissist or pure obsessive. We all possess many of the traits found in the different personality disorder types. In fact, a dimensional view of personality would be more accurate in that all of these individual traits exist in gradations. For example, some people may be more obsessive than others, but most of us probably have some degree of obsessive traits such as conscientiousness and orderliness. Similarly most of us have dependent and narcissistic traits, which vary in degree along a continuum.

The classical personality types, which are featured in DSM-IV, come from a long line of psychiatric literature dating back more than 100 years. Some basic personality types were identified in Ancient Greece, the melancholic, the sanguine, the choleric, and the phlegmatic. Today we might refer to these types as depressive, upbeat, irritable and unflappable.

The personality disorder types as currently defined may be seen as prototypes, somewhat artificial but against which we can compare individuals to determine if they fit generally within that broad category. In this chapter I want to examine some of these personality disorder types and explore how love and loss are experienced by such people, in order to enhance our understanding of the centrality of love and loss in human life.

I will start with the narcissistic personality because people with these features are often the victims of social disdain. So much so in fact, that the narcissist has been the subject of a best seller *"The Culture of Narcissism"* written by Christopher Lasch (1979). The narcissist is often reviled for his arrogance, superiority, sense of entitlement and disregard for the feelings of others. Quite a damning citation! Many readers will have worked for a boss with many narcissistic traits whose main goal within the organization appears to be self-aggrandizement and fame. Vanity pre-empts substance; sizzle is more valued than steak. Narcissistic individuals may in fact be successful visionary leaders of organizations or political parties whose own needs for admiration allow them to motivate and inspire members of the organization around a common goal. Leaders who have narcissistic traits may be very valuable particularly when an organization is in its early stages and requires a leader with charisma and energy. Propelled by the need for self-glory, narcissistic leaders can carry the organization with them but only up to a certain point. Once an organization reaches a more mature stage of day-to-day functioning, a leader with more staying power, organization skills, and commitment to hard work is required.

People with many narcissistic traits get a bad wrap because the features that are evident on the surface such as egocentricity, superiority, and belittling of others are in fact merely defences to a much deeper deficit. While a narcissistic individual may appear to be arrogant, "full of himself", and somewhat grandiose in his own self-appraisal, the inner truth is very different. For what the narcissist lacks is self-love; the narcissistic person lacks adequate self-esteem. Behind the surface bravado and boastfulness, the narcissist is insecure, feels inadequate, may loathe himself and feel isolated from true connection with others. The narcissist is a victim of inadequate attachment relationships at an early age leading to a sense of being unloved and unlovable, setting off a life time quest to counteract this inner void.

The narcissist may seek to fill this void by achieving fame and admiration in various walks of life. Film stars and other celebrities frequently exhibit narcissistic traits. They strive to be admired and loved. They crave the constant applause to maintain their limited self-esteem. However, the narcissist feels only as good as his last public performance, the well needs to be continuously refilled. The actor needs to go on stage every night to feel and hear the applause to maintain a sense of being loved. In consequence, nothing is more threatening to the narcissistic film star or actor than advancing age. This entails diminishing physical attractiveness and the accompanying loss of the public's admiration.

Narcissistic people may attempt to gain this admiration by becoming leaders in organizations, political parties and of countries. By this means they acquire steady adulation and admiration for as long as they can deliver the goods to their fawning constituents.

In truth the narcissist is rarely happy; the inner void, the lack of self-love, is only temporarily gratified. The narcissist may seek throughout life to enter into relationships that will somehow make up for the deficits of early childhood in the vain hope of providing enduring love and a sustained self-esteem. The partner of the narcissist feels used and unappreciated. She is often worn out by the constant need to reassure and bolster her spouse. Often such one-sided relationships cannot last and the partner may leave. In response to the loss of love the narcissist experiences a deep hurt; his self esteem plummets catastrophically.

Case study

Frank was a 42-year-old unemployed divorced architect, with no children. He came to therapy with feelings of emptiness and sadness. He described a lack of meaning and purpose in his life. Growing up his father was uncaring and distant. He described his mother as harsh and unsympathetic. Neither parent showed physical affection or warmth. Frank grew up craving acceptance and approval from others. He had a constant need to be validated and admired in order to maintain his fragile self-esteem. He sought this particularly in his heterosexual relationships. If he was involved in a relationship with a loving and caring woman, he felt good about himself and was successful in his chosen career. However, when these relationships ended, he quickly deflated and felt useless and worthless and saw no point or meaning to his life. At such times he would contemplate suicide by means of hanging or cutting his throat. On one such occasion, he did attempt suicide by taking an overdose of medication.

When he came to therapy, he was at a particularly low ebb after a blissful relationship of three years had come to an end with the departure of his girlfriend back to her family in Germany. In response to this loss, Frank again experienced intense sadness, emptiness and self-loathing.

Frank reported having many successful sexual relationships over the years but surprisingly said that he had great difficulty conversing with women and dating. He found the sexual relationship much easier than making small talk, chitchat and "getting to know" the other person. This is an intriguing although not unique twist to a common story.

Because of his early damaged attachment relationships, Frank was programmed to anticipate rejection and evaluation by others.

His repeated and unconscious assumption was that others would form negative evaluations of him as a person, view him as inferior and regard him as unlovable. Consequently for him the beginning of a relationship is filled with trepidation, anxiety, and fears that he would be judged and found wanting. Sometimes he would compensate for this with a grandiose boastfulness and superficial air of superiority and camaraderie. But this, like beauty, was only skin deep and inside he tended to shake with the fear of the next humiliation and rejection.

Somehow in the bedroom, these feelings like his clothes could easily be thrown off. Perhaps the physical nakedness reduced both partners to the universal level of equality: there was nothing more to hide.

People with obsessive personalities are characterized by the over zealous attention to detail, order, neatness and control of their environment. People with obsessive traits therefore have some very desirable attributes when applied to the workplace and in the professions. We would all prefer to have a physician who is obsessive and meticulous so that he does not make errors. An obsessive surgeon is reassuring: no blood vessels will be left untied and every part of the operation will be carried out with the most careful attention to detail. Schoolteachers often display strong obsessive traits, which are required for them in their didactic roles. Classes have to be ordered, course work has to be covered in set sequences and repetition is often required. The obsessive personality may be perfectionists to the point that this is self-defeating. So much attention to being perfect can lead to a fear of failure, leading to procrastination and eventually to immobilization.

Obsessive individuals tend to be highly intellectual in their outlook; the style is much more "cerebral" with reliance on logic, careful reflection and tedious systematic decision-making. People with many obsessive traits are quite detached from the emotional side of the brain, the limbic system. They are accountants rather than artists, physicians rather than massage therapists. Obsessive individuals at the best of times seem to be somewhat unaware of their feelings. They may not seem to register the emotional impact of an event and be caught up in logical analysis rather than giving vent to their feelings.

Therefore those with many obsessive traits may have difficulties when it comes to love and intimate relationships. They may not be able to access their feelings of passion and excitement and conversely may not be able to be empathic to the feelings of their lovers. Emotions and passions are dangerous to the obsessive and risk overwhelming the controls of the logical brain and his rigid conscience and moral outlook. Their response to loss of love may be muted by defences of rationalization and intellectualization.

The histrionic personality, formerly known as the "hysteric", occupies the opposite end of the spectrum to the obsessive. The histrionic stereotype is all emotion and no forethought; all passion and no contemplation. The hysteric is easily overwhelmed by the powerful forces of attachment, love and sexuality. The style of thinking of the hysteric rather than being logical and considered is often vague and fuzzy, leading to rash and counterproductive judgments. The hysteric is likely to enter into love relationships too quickly, drawn by the emotional pull and giving short shrift to potential pitfalls. The hysteric may be seen as flirtatious and enticing but lacking in depth and persistence. The hysteric responds to loss with dramatic displays of emotion which while intense may not be as enduring as one might expect!

The psychopathic or antisocial personality is characterized by extreme self-interest and total disregard for the rights or feelings of others. Other people are merely objects to be used for the benefit of the psychopath. The psychopath has no conscience. He experiences no guilt, no remorse. He can be charming and persuasive, seductive and alluring, but only to benefit himself. He is constitutionally unable to be empathic or considerate of the needs of his lover. He may restrict his wife's freedom to socialise with others and physically abuse her. He is never troubled by guilt, only by the fear of being caught and punished. The psychopath may have many lovers, but never maintains any sense of commitment to them or displays any true concern for their welfare. When he has had his fill, he will move on to his next victim. In extreme cases, the psychopath is the serial killer, the predator, who tracks his quarry to fulfil his sexual and aggressive needs. The psychopath's response to loss may be indifference or rage. The rage stems from his loss of ability to control the love object and use her as he sees fit. He may become so enraged that he contemplates homicide. Many such women partners of psychopaths are murdered each year despite "restraining orders" issued by the courts.

The borderline personality has become a cause celebre within the psychiatric field. Patients with these personality traits represent an extremely high percentage of individuals who seek help through psychiatric outpatient or inpatient services. The borderline patient represents attachment disorder, par excellence. Borderlines have extremely insecure attachment. This is reflected in dysregulation of emotions and turbulent relationships. Borderlines are so desperate to attach that they frequently throw themselves into relationships and become sexually involved in the hopes of receiving some love and affection. They crave affection. They become possessive of their partners and require constant support and reassurance. This may become overwhelming and exhausting for the partner and may lead to an eventual break-up of the relationship. In response to such rejection or abandonment, the borderline patient becomes extremely depressed and distraught and may at that point attempt suicide or other forms of self-harm.

The schizoid personality is one of extreme fragility. The schizoid person is terrified of closeness and intimacy. Again because of deranged early attachment, the schizoid person is unable to establish a mutually loving and empathic relationship. Rather he tends to be isolated, "a loner", wants to be left alone. He perceives attempts at closeness as intrusions on his very sense of himself. Such advances are accompanied by a sense of doom and impending personal annihilation. The schizoid may become a classic "hermit" or choose professions which allow him to work in isolation from other people and which do not require him to develop reciprocal affection and collaboration. Response to loss may manifest indirectly in derangements of behaviour or increased levels of psychiatric symptoms.

Paranoid personalities may well be able to develop close and intimate relationships and indeed be very empathic and sensitive to the feelings of their partners. However, the paranoid personality is prone to suspiciousness and mistrust. Jealousy is the hallmark of the paranoid personality as exemplified by Shakespeare's *Othello*. The paranoid becomes suspicious of his partner's fidelity; he begins to question and harass the partner; he can never be reassured. The partner feels persecuted and controlled. The paranoid spouse is possessive, restricting and abusive. In extreme cases, this can lead to homicide of the wife who is suspected of infidelity, or of the male who is suspected of being her lover.

People with dependent personalities may be able to develop successful relationships but because of a lack of confidence in their own abilities and worthiness may become overly reliant on their partners. They may require much reassurance that they are loved, practical support and nurturance. Over time this can be wearing to the spouse and lead to marital discord. Following loss of love the dependent personality becomes quite helpless and disabled.

Psychiatric illness

There are some psychiatric disorders that display very profound disturbances in the ability to establish mutually loving and intimate relationships. One of the most striking is that of autism, which some authors have felt may be a paradigm for disordered attachment relationships. Autism manifests early within life within the first three years. This is characterized by solitary repetitive play; the lack of ability to form a loving relationship with the parents and impairments in linguistic communication. Certainly the autistic child seems overly cerebral, somewhat rigid in style of speech and mannerisms. Unlike the borderline personality, this seems to be more profound than an attachment disorder. The autistic child may lack some of the structural elements that may be required for the normal establishment of feelings of attachment. It seems much more akin to a neurological disorder than to a psychological disorder. There are profound deficits that are not alterable by standard psychological interventions, neither are they understandable as the result of impaired attachment relationships. It may be that children with autism lack some of the underlying neural circuitry or neural connections but these are structural rather than psychological deficits.

Depression is one of the commonest psychiatric disorders. It can arise in a number of forms. Major depression is characterised by low mood, disturbances in sleep, appetite, sex drive, energy and concentration. When severe it leads to thoughts of suicide and suicide attempts. Major depression lasts on average 3 to 18 months. It may occur as single or recurrent episodes. Dysthymia is a low-grade depression that may last for years. Individuals with dysthymia have a reduced capacity to experience enjoyment and pleasure. As a result their motivation, interest in things and energy are low. It is fairly well known that one of the symptoms of depression is reduced sex drive. This can interfere with the ability to establish and maintain loving relationships. Another twist in this story is that several of the medications used to treat depression also reduce sexual drive as well as sexual performance i.e. they can cause erectile dysfunction or anorgasmia. What is less well known is that all positive feelings can be numbed or masked by depression. This includes feelings of affection and love.

Case study

Margaret was a 36-year-old married mother of three children: two daughters aged 6 years and 11 months and a son aged 4years. She presented for psychiatric treatment 11 months after the birth of her third child. She had had a low-grade post partum depression that had gone undiagnosed until 6 months after delivering a 7 lb 4 oz baby girl.

She was quite severely depressed with weepiness, insomnia, extreme fatigue and occasional thoughts of suicide but no plans or intentions to act on these thoughts. She expressed a lot of feelings of guilt and self blame which are common symptoms of depressive illness. However it was only on her second visit that she was able to reveal that she experienced no feelings of love for her children. Consequently she viewed herself as an undeserving and unworthy mother and felt her children would be better off if she were dead. She experienced some relief when her therapist carefully explained that her lack of ability to feel love towards her children was a symptom of the depression. She was informed that when she recovered from the depression, her capacity to feel love, joy and other positive emotions would return.

Bipolar disorder consists of periods of depressed mood and periods of high mood. High moods are referred to as mania or hypomania (little mania) depending on severity. During depressive episodes symptoms are very similar to those seen in major depression. In mania and hypomania there is a reversal of many symptoms: mood is elevated; energy and sex drive are greatly increased; the individual feels much more confidant and extroverted. The risk in terms of love and loss is that people who are manic or hypo manic may enter into relationships on impulse leading to major problems with their families and current spouses.

Anxiety disorders may affect the capacity to initiate relationships. In particular social anxiety is marked by shyness, fears of being judged by others or embarrassed. Such individuals may not have the nerve to ask someone out on a date.

Schizophrenia is considered one of the most serious psychiatric disorders. It includes derangements of emotions, thoughts and perceptions. Untreated the capacity to engage in close relationships is very limited. However with modern treatments the outlook is much more positive and conjugal relationships can be a reasonable aspiration for individuals diagnosed with this disease.

Posttraumatic stress disorder (PTSD) can have an enduring effect on the capacity to maintain loving relationships. A very common cause of PTSD is early childhood sexual abuse. Individuals suffering from PTSD have recurring intrusive memories of the abuse (flashbacks) and recurring nightmares. Flashbacks may be triggered by situations reminiscent of the abuse. Frequently the attempt to establish intimate sexual relationships is disturbed by intense anxiety and flashbacks. Treatment usually requires long-term psychotherapy as well as some education of the spouse or partner.

Case study

Carol was a 25-year-old supermarket cashier. She was the eldest in a sib line of three, with two younger brothers. She never knew her biological father as he had left her mother Dawn, when Carol was only six months old. Shortly thereafter Dawn entered a relationship with Ted who was the father of Carol's two brothers. Ted drank heavily and had an explosive temper. He was jealous and controlling. He often beat Dawn. When Carol was twelve, Ted began molesting her. The abuse included vaginal penetration and persisted until Carol was 16-years-old when she left home. Ted had threatened to kill her if she ever told anyone about the sexual abuse. Carol had never dated. She lived a fairly unobtrusive life: she was conscientious at work and rather meek. She liked to go to bingo on her time off. At work she was befriended by John, a good-natured 19-year-old boy who worked stocking the shelves. They began to date but quickly ran into difficulties. Every time John attempted to express any physical affection, Carol would push him away and distance herself. In therapy Carol revealed that any form of physical contact initiated by John triggered vivid and horrific memories of the sexual abuse she had undergone as a child. Therapy was long and painful. Carol was able to gingerly discuss her feelings and memories in the context of an accepting and nonjudgmental therapeutic atmosphere.

CHAPTER SIX

Deviations of love and sexual desire

Proposition #6 Disorders of sexual desire comprise the inability to establish healthy attachments simultaneously with sexual intercourse.

The terms perversion and sexual deviation are controversial and carry with them discordant views about autonomy and social behaviour. In official psychiatric classification these terms have been replaced by the term "paraphilias" which means "disorders of love". The controversies pertain to the definition of the boundaries of human sexual conduct. I will leave aside the question of what is considered "normal" sexual behaviour in contemporary society. I will start this discussion from an historical Freudian point of view without implications as to which behaviours are sanctioned in the present day. I use the Freudian metaphor because up until recently we have had no other language with which to attempt to explain the nature and deviations of man's sexual behaviour. We must remember that Freud's original aspirations were to develop a biological theory of mental functioning but because of the paucity of scientific information at the time, he was forced to develop a "metapsychological" theory of the mind. In the absence of a fundamental understanding of the underlying biology and physiology, he used the term "metapsychology" to refer to a series of conceptual constructs (e.g. ego, superego, id, drives, defences) that constitute an analogous or metaphorical parallel to underlying neurobiological processes. It is only in the last two decades that some of the underlying neurobiological workings of the brain have been elaborated. Freud grouped deviations of the sexual instinct into two categories: deviations with respect to the sexual object and deviations with respect to the sexual aim. Freud used the term "sexual object" to refer to the person who is sexually attracting; sexual aim refers to the nature of the sexual act. For Freud the normal expression of sexual behaviour was the choice of a member of the opposite sex as an object, and the joining of the genital organs, the normal aim of sexual intercourse. However, Freud goes on to say:

> "Psychoanalytic research is most decidedly opposed to any attempt at separating of homosexuals from the rest of mankind as a group of a special character … all human beings are capable of making a homosexual object choice and have, in fact, made one in their unconscious" (Freud, 1905d, p. 145).

In fact, Freud believed that humans have a bisexual disposition and that the choice of male or female object is only determined later in development as a result of many factors including both constitutional (inborn) and a number of "accidental" factors, referring to family and environmental circumstances. Additionally Freud noted the difficulties in drawing a sharp line between what is physiological and what is pathological. He postulated that the perversions were on a continuum with normal sexual behaviour.

> "No healthy person, it appears, can fail to make some addition that might be called perverse to the normal sexual aim; and the universality of this finding is in itself enough to show how inappropriate it is to use the word perversion as a term of reproach" (Freud, 1905d, p. 160).

The main forms of paraphilias include the following:

Fetishism is the need to achieve sexual arousal by means of a non-genital body part or inanimate object. Freud remarked that kissing, which is contact "between the mucous membrane of the lips of the two people concerned" (Freud, 1905d, p. 150), is highly valued even though the regions of the body involved do not form part of the sexual system. He realized that any region of the skin or mucous membrane is capable of being the focus of sexual excitation in addition to the genitals: the mouth, anus, and breasts. Yet it is still perplexing that a part of the body or a material object can become infused with sexual charge and cause sexual arousal. Such objects do not facilitate the supposed primary sexual aim of genital union.

In the classical Freudian view, it was believed that the basis for fetishism was the fear of castration and that the fetish object was a symbolic representation of the genitals, e.g. the foot, shoe or slipper, as symbols of the penis or female genitalia; fur and velvet being symbolic of pubic hair.

One could conceive of fetishism as the outgrowth of classical conditioning i.e. the association in time of these objects with sexual arousal in the same way that Pavlov's bell became associated with food. An alternative theory is that fetish objects contain exaggerated attributes of normal sexual forms and textures e.g. leather as a form of "super" skin: firm, smooth, strong.

Smell, touching, and looking are also capable of provoking sexual excitation. Conventionally it is believed that men are more responsible to visual stimulation, women more responsive to tactile stimulation. The role of smell in our own day is readily apparent in the vast cosmetic perfume industry. Visual sexual stimuli abound in art, advertising and pornography. Too much preoccupation with these aspects of sexuality is regarded as deviant if

"... instead of being preparatory to the normal sexual aim, it supplants it" (Freud, 1905d, p. 157).

In object relations terms, the use of a fetish object may protect against fears of loss of self. Genital union requires a "letting-go", a dissolution of boundaries. The fetishist unconsciously fears he will become engulfed and lose all sense and control of himself if he engages in sexual intercourse.

What seems striking in this and other paraphilias is the absence of loving attachment to another person. The sexual object is an "object" in the non-technical sense i.e. a "thing". The fetishist is unable to attach to his partner, but rather relates to a part of the other's body. He has difficulty combining sexual intercourse with a loving attachment relationship.

Exhibitionism is defined in the Diagnostic and Statistical Manual of the American Psychiatric Association (DSM-IV) as intense sexually arousing fantasies, urges or behaviours involving the exposure of the genitals to an unsuspecting stranger. This is accompanied by sexual excitement and may be a means of creating fear and domination from a safe distance. The exhibitionist is unable to get close enough to develop an attachment to the object of his sexual desires.

Voyeurism is the converse of exhibitionism. The reaction of fear and shock in the victims of exhibitionism reassure the individual that he retains his masculine power and potency. In Freudian terms it reduces the anxiety associated with the unconscious fear of castration. Such individuals may have felt humiliated by women during the course of their development and this behaviour may be a form of revenge. Feelings of humiliation and inadequacy may be the main components of the exhibitionist's object relations. The voyeur may be too paralyzed by anxiety and fears to attach and simultaneously engage in open sexual relations. He therefore watches at a safe distance. Both exhibitionism and voyeurism have been legitimized in our society in the vast pornographic industry.

The human appetite for sadism and masochism is particularly mystifying and in many respects is very disturbing to conventional social mores. Sadism is the desire to inflict pain upon the sexual object, masochism is the desire to have pain inflicted upon oneself by the sexual object. We are confused and unsettled by the conjunction of pain and pleasure and until recently have had no explanation for this strange result of human evolution.

Sexual masochism is defined as current fantasies, sexual urges or behaviours involving the act of being humiliated, beaten, bound or otherwise made to suffer. There has been the assumption that masochistic patients are re-enacting childhood experiences of abuse. For some, shame and guilt around sexuality may restrict them to experiencing sexual arousal only when punishment is included. For others submission to the infliction of pain may have been the only means by which they had been able to maintain any form of attachment: an abusive relationship may be better than none at all.

We cannot discuss the subject of sexual deviations or sexual variations without some reference to the "phallic mother." In psychoanalysis this refers to a fantasy of a woman endowed with a phallus. In more general symbolic terms, it refers to the attribution to a woman of the power and strength normally considered to be "masculine" characteristics. Such women are exemplified in the form of the "dominatrix" who uses the symbols of power and cruelty (black leather has a special place in their armamentaria). Perhaps also in this regard may be the attraction to some, of transgendered men, so-called "shemales", who maintain sexual characteristics of both genders i.e. large female breasts along with a penis.

Sexual sadism comprises sexual fantasies, urges or behaviours that involve inflicting psychological or physical pain on others. The sexual sadist achieves sexual arousal through the exercise of aggression and violence. Again sadistic individuals may be acting out situations that they endured in their own lives that resulted in a compulsion for revenge and a need for mastery and domination.

Feminist groups have often made the point that crimes of sexual assault are about power and domination not about sexuality. This is a false dichotomy. A certain amount of submission and aggression are part of all sexual relationships and neurobiologically the location of sexual and aggressive drives may be intertwined at some points. The sexual predator seeks to dominate and control *in order to* achieve sexual arousal and orgasm.

These colourful psychoanalytic metaphors leave us with an incomplete understanding and we must turn now to a more recent and broader view of human evolution to find some rational explanation for these behaviours.

Sadism and masochism involve not only the infliction of physical pain but also of psychological pain in the form of degradation and humiliation. This may link us to the role of dominance and submission in our mammalian and human ancestors. Dominant male behaviour for example among baboons is associated with control and choice over the female members of the troop and therefore confers an evolutionary advantage for the dominant males. Conversely it is important for a male who has been defeated in contests over reproductive rights to be able to display submissiveness in order not to be killed.

For the sadist and masochist sexual resolution is dependent upon the infliction of physical or mental pain. Freud commented on the "intimate connection between cruelty and the sexual instinct ..."

(Freud, 1905d, p. 159), throughout the history of human civilization. He speculated on a connection to cannibalistic desires (the movie "*Silence Of the Lambs*" would lend support to this thesis).

Victor Nell (2006) in a masterful review of the subject of cruelty opens up some avenues of enlightenment on this extraordinary topic. He defines cruelty as the "deliberate infliction or physical or psychological pain on a living creature". What he finds most disturbing in this is the frequent evidence of "delight" experienced by the perpetrators of such cruelty. Cruelty is ever present in our world in wars and massacres and in the activities of interrogators who use torture and in the attraction of gory and blood thirsty media representations, in cinema and in sport.

Nell postulates that cruelty must have some survival benefits in terms of human evolution and traces the origin of such behaviour to our past as predatory hunters. This is still evident in our evolutionary ancestors, mammals and the primates who continue to hunt and kill for food. Nell identifies a "pain-blood-death complex" which is triggered by stalking the prey, the excruciating terror, the vicious struggle, the wounding of the prey and the shedding of the blood, the eating of the prey often while it is still alive and struggling.

Ten thousand years ago our human ancestors lived in small bands of hunter-gatherers. These groups hunted together and shared the spoils. Group members were loyal to each other and suspicious of outsiders. Both our hunting and killing instincts are "hard wired" in the more primitive areas of our brains. The pleasure associated with gorging on the kill became connected with the feelings evoked by the hunt itself and the exercise of aggression and cruelty in the process of killing.

The attraction of blood sports such as fox and deer hunting, boxing and even of football are expressions of those primordial hunting instincts. Not only do we all contain within us the potential for aggression and even cruelty, but we also carry a certain fascination in watching acts of killing and cruelty. One only has to undertake a quick review of popular movies to be impressed by the incessant images of bloody assassinations, torture and war.

The human attraction to watching blood and death was spectacularly evident in the gladiator games of the Roman Coliseum.

Bullfighting and extreme sports are further confirmation of these tendencies.

The neurobiological basis for predatory aggression may be mediated by the neurobiological system that underlies the actions of exploration and the search for food. Dopamine pathways from the midbrain and the ventral tegmental area to the nucleus accumbens form the underlying circuitry for exploratory and search behaviours. In some species this manifests as foraging and in others as predatory stalking. The pleasure and satisfaction that follow the kill and feeding are mediated by dopamine and opioid systems. Opioids are released during the killing-feeding cycle and may be further enhanced in response to bodily injuries incurred in the course of the struggle. The act of hunting, killing, and feeding brings together the predatory instincts with the pleasurable rewards. Embroiled in this mixture there is also the ingredient of sexual arousal and excitement. The same circumstances arouse both aggressive and sexual drives.

There is another link between these two instinctual components: it is the aggressive and successful male hunter who achieves dominance in the group and who both attracts and gets preferential access to females. This pattern is seen in humans by the "fatal attraction" between certain women and imprisoned psychopathic killers.

In childhood, rough-and-tumble play is an expression of and a precursor to the exercise of the predatory instinct.

The predatory cycle may be triggered by hunger and enhanced by the sight of the prey. The prey's attempt to flee, further stimulates the hunter. The prey struggles and fearful vocalizations further arouse and energize the predator and the sight, smell and taste of blood, becomes conditioned to the reward system. These stimuli because of their association with the rewards of consuming the prey and satiation can become themselves independently reinforcers of human behaviour. This is the so-called "blood lust".

As humans evolved socially and culturally, there has been an attempt to override the expression of aggression and cruelty by means of social and legal sanctions and the development of civilized society. This is an attempt by the higher brain, the frontal neocortex, to override the primitive impulses of our mammalian limbic system. In Freudian terms it is the battle between the "superego" (our internalized social conscience) and our unconscious "id" instincts of aggression and sexuality. Clearly we have lost the battle as is evident by the perpetuation of war throughout the centuries and continents of the human world. Likewise, it is clear in individual behaviour that in some, the predatory and sadistic instincts are too strong, leading to acts of sexual assault, rape and serial sexual killing.

Seen in this light, the existence of sadism becomes much more understandable. Masochism includes the same primitive urges only directed inwardly rather than outwardly. It is in these same neuro-circuits that Freud's death instinct may lurk.

CHAPTER SEVEN

Loss

Proposition #7 The intensity of loss and grief is directly proportional to the intensity of the attachment bond and its felt component, love.

Separation from the one we love propels us into a state of all-consuming sorrow. Loss of the love object gives rise to the same emotions that occur when an infant is separated from its primary attachment, "We are never so defenceless against suffering as when we love, never so forlornly unhappy as when we have lost our love object or its love" (Freud, 1930a, p. 82). Freud determined that grief is the reaction specific to object loss and occurs following the loss. In contrast anxiety is a response to the prospect of losing the love object and arises when there is a threat to the continuation of the relationship. These dynamics are masterfully conveyed by Shakespeare in *"Romeo and Juliet"*, the couple that inspired the title of this book:

> "Wilt thou be gone? It is not yet near day.
> It was the nightingale, and not the lark,"
>
> (Act 3 scene 5)

We can hear the apprehension in Juliet's voice as she tries to postpone Romeo's departure which must come at the break of day. In the ensuing lines of the tragedy, there is a rising level of anxiety as both Juliet and Romeo are forced to face the inevitability of their separation. Juliet urgently implores Romeo not to go and he in turn is prepared to risk death in order to remain with her:

> "Let me be ta'en; let me be put to death ...
> I have more care to stay than will to go.
> Come death and welcome. Juliet wills it so."
>
> (Act 3 Scene 5)

In these passages there is a notable juxtaposition of leaving and dying. Separation from the beloved one is for Romeo and many others worse than death. It is this link between love, loss and desire to die that I will explore in this and the following chapter.

In attachment terms it is the secure base which allows the infant to develop and become autonomous. The loss of the secure base results in protest, despair and detachment. In adulthood the same pattern is evident in response to the loss of love. This entails a loss of the feeling of being loved, a loss of the feeling of being worthy, and a loss of feeling of being safe. What remains is a feeling of inner desolation, of utter aloneness.

Anxiety, fear, and apprehension are the primary felt emotions when relationships become strained or under threat of break up. Anxiety is an emotion of anticipation; it is directed towards a potential future eventuality. The components of anxiety include worry, tension, edginess, jitteriness "butterflies" or "gut wrenching". Worry may consist of ruminations: repetitive, intense anxious thoughts focused obsessively on the object of love.

There are also physiological changes that accompany the emotion of anxiety: increased heart rate and respirations; feelings of heat or cold (chills, goose bumps), light-headedness, nausea, diarrhoea. If the threatened loss actually ensues the emotional response consists of extreme sorrow and despair.

During the early weeks following the loss, the person affected may not be able to accept that the loss has really taken place; the defence of denial may come into play, manifested in expressions of disbelief. There is an intense urge to make contact with the person who has left. There is an extreme longing and a restless searching for the lost object. We become filled with great sadness and uncontained crying. Loss shatters our sense of self. There is both an external loss and a corresponding loss of internal balance. When we leave or are left by those we love it feels as if something dies inside us. Something is missing; we feel empty. In the words of *"Chanson de l' Adieu"*: (*Song of Farewell*), an old French song, *"Partir c'est mourir un peu"*, which in English translates to:

> Parting is to die a little
> Dying from what we love
> We leave a little of ourselves
> In every hour and in every place.

Loss of the lover, the primary attachment figure, whether by separation or death subsumes a loss of self. In chapter three I demonstrated that our sense of identity grows out of the dyadic relationship between the infant and its attachment figures. Similarly it follows that as adults, the ongoing maintenance of our sense of identity depends on ongoing dyadic relationships. In object relations terms we have internalized both good and bad objects that combine to produce our sense of self and our personality. The sense of self is maintained by ongoing interpersonal interactions particularly those with the new primary attachment figure, the spouse or lover.

In response to loss we feel as if we are dying. This is so because something within us does die. Our internal self and object representations undergo a shift because the attachment relationship is no longer available to sustain them. The loss of the internalized object is felt as an inner void. The more intense the specific attachment was, the greater is the pain of the loss.

D. H. Lawrence beautifully depicts the effect of loss on our sense of identity in his poem *"Humiliation"*:

> " What should I do if you were gone again so soon?
> What should I look for?
> Where should I go?
> What should I be, I myself
> 'I' ?
> What would it mean, this
> 'I' ?

Do not leave me.

And:

"I would bear the pain
But always, strong, unremitting
It would make me not me.
The thing with my body that would go on living
Would not be me.
Neither life nor death could help".

(Lawrence 1964)

Lawrence intuitively reveals the intimate link between loss of the love object and the loss of his sense of identity. Great art illustrates the same themes. For example in Munch's "*Young woman on the Shore*" (Figure 3) we can perceive what loss and loneliness feel like. The young woman is dressed in white which gives emphasis to her solitariness. Her back is to us, so we cannot see her facial expression. She is surrounded by the pale melancholy blue of the sea. The painting conveys a feeling of great sadness and emptiness:

Munch Museum, Oslo

Figure 3. Young woman on the Shore.

In clinical psychiatry relationship break-ups are not an infrequent presentation. Men and woman of any age many seek psychiatric help while they are in the midst of an acute crisis of separation. With the sorrow and despair, there may be marked agitation, pacing and restlessness. And when most despairing the person may come to feel that he cannot go on living because the pain of loss is unendurable. Following the sorrow, feelings of anger and rage emerge. Homicidal urges may be directed towards the partner who has left or at the new lover. Violent jealousy is most often seen in young adult males who are quick to anger and who often want to inflict retaliation. There then follows a stage of grieving that may last from months to years. In some cases this may never be resolved.

Case study

Julie was a 29-year-old emergency room nurse. She was competent, attractive and had a vivacious flair. Her demeanour altered dramatically when her boyfriend of five years left her for another woman. At worked she appeared subdued and preoccupied. Her confidant and efficient air was replaced by hesitancy and indecisiveness. One evening she ran out of a patient's room and began to sob bitterly. She was seen for urgent psychiatric evaluation. She described feelings of sadness and grief in response to the break up. She thought almost constantly about her boyfriend. She had difficulty getting to sleep and woke several times during the night. She felt tired all the time. Her appetite was poor and her weight had dropped 9 lbs since her boyfriend had left 4 weeks earlier. She could not concentrate on her work and experienced no enjoyment with anything. She felt terribly alone.

For many months Julie wept bitterly in her therapy sessions. She questioned the meaning of her life and struggled to resist urges to end her life. She ventilated her sorrow and grief in the course of therapy gradually letting go of the attachment feelings towards her former boyfriend. Through her other attachments and the secure base of therapy she eventually re-established her sense of her self and her confidence to once again face the outside world.

In therapy the process of grieving involves the expression of memories and feelings about the lost love object in the presence of an accepting and non-judgmental therapist. Unrealistic hopes of reunion must be gently challenged. With time there is healing and acceptance of the new status quo. Healing is not a linear process and the phases of despair, anger and acceptance overlap and shift back and forth. A broken relationship is analogous to having a broken leg. At first there is much "bleeding" and pain; gradually there is some healing and the bones begin to grow back together. However if any stress is put on the wound, in the case of the leg by attempting to walk too early, or in the case of lost love by talking with the departed lover too soon, the wounds reopen with a further round of bleeding and pain, grief and anger.

Canadian poet Sheree Fitch captures the despondency of life without love and tries to compensate by writing a poem she has titled *"When Flesh Suggests"*:

> "I thought I'd learned to live
> without caress of breasts
> I pull the flannel quickly
> back across my flesh
> to cover up
> the moment
> but the flannel brushes soft
> against my nipple
> my skin is hungry
> there is nothing I can do
> but write a poem
> after dancing
> it's the next best thing
> to making love"
>
> S. Fitch, *In This House Are Many Women* (1993)

Case study

Mark was a 27-year-old man who lived in a small rural town and worked in a meat packing plant. He and his girlfriend Shona had lived together for two and a half years. She worked as a waitress in a bar. He was prone to be short-tempered and possessive. He drank moderately heavily, smoked marijuana a couple of times a week, and occasionally used cocaine. After work he often demanded to know if she had flirted with any of her customers in the bar. He used to yell or smash objects against the wall. Finally Shona felt she could no longer tolerate this behaviour and moved out. Mark was enraged and distraught. The day after Shona had left he got into an altercation at work. As he was leaving work he shouted out that he "didn't give a damn" and might as well ride his motorcycle into a transport truck on the highway. At 1am that night he contacted Shona by phone and told her that no other man was ever going to have her because he would kill her first and then himself. Shona was scared and phoned Mark's best friend. He suggested she call the police. The police went to Mark's home and persuaded him to accompany them to the local hospital emergency room. There he was assessed by the psychiatrist on call and held overnight for observation. The following day he had sobered up and denied that he would follow through on either the homicidal or suicidal threats. He was released with a promise to follow up at a psychiatric clinic the following Tuesday. He kept this commitment and was seen at the clinic by a therapist. He was weepy and angry. He ventilated his feelings of extreme sadness. He felt very abandoned. At points in the interview he appealed for help to get Shona back. At other times he raised his voice and swore about "how that fucking bitch could do this to me".

By the end of the hour and a half interview Mark was more settled. He stated that he knew suicide was not the answer. He agreed that he must keep going to work and living his life. He expressed the hope that eventually Shona would realise she had made a mistake and come back to him.

The following Monday morning the therapist received a phone call from the local police informing her that Mark was dead. He had been at a party on Saturday night; he had drunk heavily and left at midnight. On Sunday afternoon he was found hanging in the basement by his landlord.

For men like Mark, the loss of the love object is too damaging to their sense of self. The need to possess the love object is so intense that they are constantly plagued by jealous thoughts. They seek to control the love object by demanding an accounting of their whereabouts at all times. Their existence depends on the immediate availability of the love object to provide a sense of wholeness. Their extreme reliance on the partner to maintain their sense of identity is masked by a defensive tough machismo exterior. When the love object is truly lost and the defences fail, the outcome can be fatal!

To compensate for the loss of our love object we cling on to the notion that part of the object will always remain internalized as an inner representation. In a wider sense the love object has affected our inner sense of who we are. Popular songs attest to this feeling that "you will always be part of me". There is the wistful longing for reconnection.

I will conclude this chapter with Kahlil Gibran's masterpiece for no one else has so exquisitely captured the pain of separation and the dreamed for wish for reunion:

> "Farewell to you and the youth I have spent with you.
> It was but yesterday we met in a dream.
> You have sung to me in my aloneness, and I of your longings have built a tower in the sky.
> But now our sleep has fled and our dream is over, and it is no longer dawn.
> The noontide is upon us and our half waking has turned to fuller day, and we must part.
> If in the twilight of memory we should meet once more, we shall speak again together and you shall sing to me a deeper song.
> And if our hands should meet in another dream, we shall build another tower in the sky."
>
> Gibran, (1978)

CHAPTER EIGHT

Suicide

Proposition #8 The death instinct exerts its effects when key
attachments are lost.

Suicide can be the final act that follows the dance of love and
loss. Suicide is the deliberate act of ending one's life, literally
"self-murder". Albert Camus in the "*The Myth of Sisyphus*"
confronting the absurdity of life, wrote that there is "but one serious
philosophic problem and that is suicide"(Camus, 1991, p. 3).

When a suicide attempt results in the individual's death it is
described as a "completed suicide". This is preferable to the descrip-
tion "successful suicide" which is a contradiction that fails to convey
the actual horror of the event. Suicide is the ultimate form of self-
injury but there are other gradations. In psychiatric practice we distinguish individuals who inflict pain on themselves but who do not
intend to kill themselves. Infliction of pain may take many forms,
cutting, burning, scalding, banging. Such behaviours are more
common in individuals who have experienced physical, sexual or
psychological abuse in childhood. Such abuse can give rise to self-
hatred and a craving for self-punishment. Cutting, in particular, is
very common. Such individuals may repeatedly cut their arms, the

back of their legs or thighs. The cuts are usually superficial and not life threatening. Patients with more intense self-loathing may cut more deeply which increases the pain level and flow of blood. Some patients have told me that they need to cut deep in order to see the blood; it is only then that they experience a sense of relief.

All of these patients can clearly articulate that their intent is not to end their lives but rather to experience the pain and the subsequent effects of the pain. They describe that after inflicting the self harm, there is an experience of relaxation, a decrease in tension and even a sense of soothing. This initially quite puzzling behaviour makes more sense if we recall that the body has its own internal painkillers, the endogenous opiates. The principal group of these are the endorphins which are released following injury or the infliction of pain. Endorphins have a calming and soothing effect. Perhaps this is one of the mechanisms that underlies the pain-relieving effects of acupuncture.

This form of self-harm is very different from the deliberate act of trying to kill oneself. The methods used may be similar but the intent is very different. Suicidal patients often slash their wrists with a razor or knife but they can clearly express their desire to die.

The attempt may or may not succeed. This will depend on whether or not a lethal method is chosen and whether or not there is a chance of rescue. Lethal methods include shooting, hanging, asphyxiation, jumping from a height, crashing a car, jumping in front of a subway train, and ingesting poisonous substances. The choice of such lethal methods reduces the chances of rescue and medical resuscitation.

Overdosing with medication is one of the commonest forms of attempted suicide. This is because of the ready availability of prescribed or over-the-counter drugs. Because it takes some time for the medications to exert their toxic effects, there is a much greater opportunity for rescue. The interval between the time the pills are swallowed and the time they begin to exert their effects, gives the individual a chance to have second thoughts and reach out for help or call an ambulance. In the event of an overdose, medical intervention can be very effective with the use of life sustaining technologies such as assisted respiratory ventilation and renal dialysis.

In considering suicide we are faced with a paradox: if the most basic of human drives is self-preservation, how can we come to understand the occurrence of suicide? Why is it that more than the loss of sustenance or shelter it is the loss of love that gives rise to the self-destructive impulse? This is an enigma that contradicts common sense. Evolution is based on the survival of the fittest so what evolutionary advantage could suicide confer on the individual? One would expect that in the course of evolution, the tendency towards suicide would be eliminated by the process of natural selection. Only those that survive can breed and perpetuate their DNA. Those that take their own lives would appear to have a lesser chance of passing on their genes to offspring. Furthermore can the enigma of suicide shed any light on our question posed at the beginning of this book: "What is the meaning or purpose of human existence"? The answer to both these questions lies within the nature of attachment relationships. Both are explained by the connection between love and loss.

This connection between love, loss, and suicide is evident in our poetry, our songs, and literature. It forcefully occurs with wrenching acuity in *"Romeo and Juliet"*, *"Madame Butterfly"* and *"Anna Karenina"*. As we have seen in chapter seven, D.H. Lawrence questions his very existence when his beloved is about to leave:

> "What should I be, I myself
> 'I'?
> What would it mean, this
> 'I'?
> Do not leave me."

Lawrence knows from his own experience that his sense of himself will shatter if his lover abandons him. Somehow his identity cannot be sustained if she departs. As we have seen in chapter three, this is because our sense of identity is intimately related to our primary attachment objects. In psychiatric practice, the loss of a loved one is one of the most common precipitating events to a suicide attempt. For young women, the end of a relationship with a boyfriend can lead to a suicide attempt, most frequently by means of an overdose or wrist-cutting. For young men, the loss of a spouse can lead to more violent methods: death by firearms or hanging.

One of the most accessible accounts of a completed suicide is that of the famous American poet Sylvia Plath who killed herself by gas asphyxiation in London in February 1963. This is recounted in unusual and sensitive detail by A. Alvarez in *"The Savage God"* (1974). I have often used this reading in tutorials with medical students. The account of a completed suicide of a mother of two young children, is powerful and shocking. It quickly attunes the students to the fact that psychiatry is about life and loss, love and death. Plath's father, a professor of Biology in Boston, had died when she was nine. She separated from her husband Ted Hughes about six months before her death after he had become involved in an affair with Assia Wevill who worked at a London advertising company. Plath had made suicide attempts prior to her marriage to Hughes.

In her poem *"Lady Lazarus"* she compares herself to a cat with nine lives and says that she had attempted suicide three times in her life.

It is well established clinically that the risk of completed suicide is higher among those who have made previous attempts. Sylvia writes in the same poem that dying is an "art":

"... I do it exceptionally well"

A few day before her death she wrote the poem "Edge" which has a serene finality:

"Her dead
Body wears the smile of accomplishment ..."

Alvarez argues that Plath did not intend to kill herself but I disagree.

On reading *"Edge"* one can be in no doubt that the risk of suicide is high. Plath made careful preparations to ensure she would die: sealing the room to ensure the gas from the oven would not seep out. The chances of rescue were low. Plath had made previous attempts. The death of her father when she was nine was an enormously significant predisposing loss. In her poem *"Daddy"* she describes her desire to be re-united with him:

"At twenty I tried to die
And get back, back, back to you ..."

A lingering postpartum depression was also a factor. However by far the most powerful determinant was the end of her relationship with her husband Ted Hughes. It was the loss of her primary attachment figure that made her life unbearable and caused her to end it.

I have used poetry frequently throughout this work and indeed the title of this book is an example of the poetic genius of Shakespeare. I have not posed, until now, the question as to why poetry is so relevant to my topic. Poetry and music share an uncanny ability to give expression to our emotions. In chapter four I have said that music is the language of the emotions, the language of our limbic systems. Poetry gets its potency from its rhythmic structure and as such it is able to invoke and represent our deepest emotions. It is love that is pre-eminent among all those emotions.

In an intriguing account of the work of five poets Andrew Brink has proposed that poetry is a means of symbolic repair in the face of object loss:

> "Poetry is seen to act as a retrieval system that calls back deepest feelings to order and to make some sense of them ..." (Brink, 1977, p. 3).

All of the poets studied by Brink had experienced early loss of parents. The creative urge of poets, according to Brink is an attempt to stave off dejection and repair the void left by object loss. Brink notes that many of Plath's poems "illustrate inner desolation intensifying itself in the absence of needed objects of which the supply is inadequate." (Brink, 1977, p. 228). He says that her poems reveal:

> "an empty core, a core surrounded by grief and potential violence for the time being deflected into verse." (Brink, 1977, p. 228).

Brink points to the break-up of her marriage to Ted Hughes as being the critical loss. But Plath did not succeed in repairing herself with her poetry. The losses and inner emptiness were too deep. For Plath, says Brink, nothing was "exorcised ... by poetry." (Brink, 1977, p. 236). There was no "reparative good object" (Brink, 1977, p. 236) to replace those that were lost, that could save Plath from self-destruction.

We are ourselves because we have internalized representations of the important people in our lives, the primary love objects. In a parallel process our identities are sustained because we continue to engage in dyadic relationships. Attachment is crucial for our survival. This is literally true when we are infants. It is psychologically true when we are adults. When attachment is lost the infant faces the threat of predators and annihilation. As adults we lose the bonds that sustain our psychological existence. We become psychologically crippled. In evolutionary terms we become a burden to our social group. Self-murder in these circumstances enhances the survival of the group.

Suicide is a manifestation of an inner destructive drive. In *"Beyond the Pleasure Principle"* Freud put forward the idea of a death instinct. In 1920 Schopenhauer had postulated that "death is the goal of life" (Jones, 1957, p. 273). Freud's thinking may have been strongly influenced by the aggression, sadism, and brutality of the First World War. But this begs the question. If love is central in human life how do we account for the existence of war, destruction, hate, genocide none of which have been eradicated despite five thousand years of "civilization". On the contrary we could regard war as the normative state in human society punctuated by short episodes of peace. Thanatos is the death instinct, a force that degrades, de-differentiates and destroys. It reduces complication to achieve a state of entropy. "The aim of all life is death" (Freud, 1920). The death instinct is the tendency of living matter to return to the inanimate state. Freud continues in his analysis of human culture, that this struggle is what all life essentially consists of:

> "In all that follows, I take up the standpoint that the tendency
> to aggression is an innate, independent, instinctual disposition
> in man ..." (Freud, 1930a, p. 122).

There is within in us, side by side with the impulse to attach, its nemesis, the human capacity for aggression and murder. Freud states "This instinct of aggression is the derivative and main representative of the death instinct we have found along side of Eros, sharing his rule over the Earth. And now it seems to me the meaning of the evolution of culture is no longer a riddle to us. It must present to us the struggle between Eros and death, between the instincts of life and the instincts of destruction, as it works itself out in the human species" (Freud, 1930a, p. 122).

Instincts are biological imperatives. Eros, the life instinct, is a metaphor for a force that binds together the elements of human existence. It operates through sexual union and love. Eros stands for DNA, evolution, combining, growth and reproduction. Eros leads to the joining of elements together to form a unity; a creative force that leads to the emergence of a more complex synthesis.

Human life evolves through the exchange and combination of genetic DNA. The combination leads to something new by means of the merger of genetic material.

In chapter four I stated that envy was a primary emotion. I can now elaborate on this and state that Melanie Klein believed that envy is a manifestation of the death instinct. The infant is faced with the annihilating terror of the death instinct in the form of self-destructiveness. It combats this by directing the destructiveness toward another object; in the first instance this is the mother and her food-giving breast.

The Death Instinct is not a popular concept and has been rejected by most schools of psychotherapy. The principle exception to this is the Kleinian school of psychoanalysis comprising the adherents of the views of Melanie Klein. It is not a concept that forms any part of scientific theory. Yet the idea of a death instinct fills a gap in our understanding of much human psychology and sociology. We have few useful theories to explain the persistence of war throughout human history. In our own times the suicide bombers have challenged our hitherto anaemic attempts to understand this. Like death itself, any deliberations about the death instinct have been banished from the forefront of our consciousnesses. Such talk is too dangerous for us. It poses too much of a challenge to our comforting ideologies and threatens our sense of deluded equanimity.

Metaphorically we can say that the loss of the primary object alters the balance between the life and death instincts, between Eros and Thanatos. When the death instinct is stronger, suicide ensues.

CHAPTER NINE

Meaning of time as a prelude to meaning

Proposition #9 Time is relative; acceleration of time is associated with alienation; expansion of time is asso- ' ciated with authenticity.

The universe began over 13 billion years ago, one-trillionth of a second after the Big Bang. Such time spans are beyond the range of human comprehension. Within this framework the existence of humans as a species is infinitesimally insignificant. The span of a human life whether of 7 years or 70, is almost irrelevant from the perspective of cosmic time. The notion of time itself is mysterious and has defied definition by ancient Greek philosophers as well as by present day astrophysicists. We feel that time flows inexorably. But if so what is actually flowing?

In the world of Newton, the occurrence of one event "A" can be clearly defined in relation to the occurrence of a later second event "B". The interval between event "A" and event "B" is well demarcated and absolute. If this interval is zero, events "A" and "B" are said to be simultaneous.

Einstein's Theory of Relativity shattered the intuitively sound Newtonian framework. In Relativity the temporal interval between

89

two points is not absolute and depends on the observer's frame of reference. Within one frame of reference event B will appear to follow event A. From another frame of reference in a different part of the universe, event A will appear to follow event B and within another A and B will occur simultaneously!

We think of time in terms of past, present and future. The past is that which has been but no longer exists, the future is a potential that has not yet come into being. Practically therefore, it is only the present that exists. This view is known as "presentism". An alternative view accepts that both the past and the present have reality but that the future remains only a possibility. This view is known as "possibilism". This may be closer to our day-to-day experience of the passage of time. From the point of view of relativity, however, there are no differences between the past, present and the future. What is seen as past and what is seen as future depends merely on the observer's location in time and space. The light that we see from distant stars left those stars millions of years ago. When the light reaches our retina we are seeing stars as they were millions of years in the past but for us it is an experience in the present. Time only exists from the point of view and from the experience of the observer. In the words of the poet T. S. Eliot (1942):

> "The end precedes the beginning,
> and the end and the beginning were always there".

There is no before and after. There is no beginning or end to what is in the universe; all that changes is the point of view of the observer. I would like to emphasize this last sentence because although the viewpoints of physicists and psychologists may seem very different, there are points of convergence. On the surface the day-to-day appreciation of time is obviously very different from that of Einstein in his theory of Special Relativity but this may not always be the case. To appreciate this I will elaborate on the nature of the human experience of time.

Within our psychological perception of time, we are conscious of a sense of duration, the interval between one event and another. We are able to appreciate that events may or may not occur simultaneously; there appears to be an order to events, that is, there is a past and a present and we can anticipate a future.

Time for us is intrinsically related to memory. Eric Kandel (2006), the Nobel Prize winning psychiatrist and neuroscientist quotes Tennessee Williams:

> "Has it ever struck you … that life is all memory, except for the one present moment that goes by so quickly you hardly catch it going? It is really all memory … except for each passing moment" (Kandel, 2006, p. 281).
>
> Kandel goes on to say that "for all of us explicit memory makes it possible to leap across space and time and conjure up events and emotional states that have vanished into the past, yet somehow continue to live on in our minds" (Kandel, 2006, p. 281).

Salvador Dali captures some of these feelings in his 1931 painting *"The Persistence of Memory"*. There is an evocation of timelessness in this painting, even of stagnation, time standing still. This is conveyed by the desolate landscape and the dilatation and curvature of the clocks.

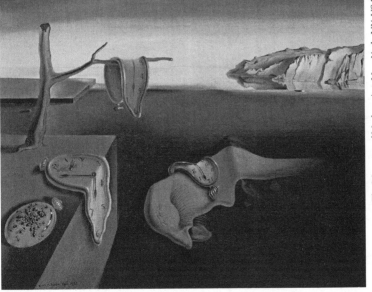

The Museum of Modern Art, New York, NY, USA

Figure 4. Salvador Dali The Persistence of Memory.

Eugene O'Neill in *"Long Day's Journey into Night"* wrote:

"The past is the present, isn't it? It is the future too."

The past is the present, continuously vanishing; the future is that which is continuously becoming present. Again, T. S. Eliot (1942) in his *"Four Quartets"* says:

"Time present and time past
are both perhaps present in time future"

Eliot poetically is saying much the same thing as Kandel and this in turn is not far off from Einstein's relativistic view. This is the point I want to underscore. The concept and experience of time is relative. It follows then that within this wider perspective, it is of limited importance how long any of us lives. Duration as a measure of life is immaterial. Duration has no intrinsic value. The life of a young soldier struck down in battle at age twenty is not less significant than the life of an 85-year-old man who dies from Alzheimer's disease. The Romans used to say that those whom the gods favour die young. Duration of time is an arbitrary construct dependent on the frame of reference. What matters is not the duration of life but some other characteristic.

Spinoza, the 17th century Jewish philosopher, proposed that man should live "sub specie aeternitatis", within the context of eternity. Rolo May in *"Man's Search for Himself"* remarks that eternity is not a given quantity of time, it is something that transcends time. The "eternal" is a way of relating to life not a succession of "tomorrows". May says that the experience of eternity will be found in how one relates to each given moment—or not at all. The experience of eternity is derived from a mode of relating as we will see when we come to consider Martin Buber in chapter eleven.

Could it be that the experience of eternity occurs when we somehow escape from the subjective awareness of time? Perhaps this is why all of the great religions attempt to sanctify time and to designate special dates for commemoration and dedication.

Immortality

In the gym you will see the strained faces of those racing on the treadmill trying to escape the ravages of time and the unavoidable progression to life's end. The race on the treadmill leads nowhere, it is just a repeating circle of rubber and metal. We cannot outrun our fate or the inevitability of our mortality. The quest for youth, health and longevity at best might postpone the destiny that all of us must accept. Again, T. S. Eliot (1922):

> "He who was living is now dead
> We who were living are now dying"
>
> (The Wasteland)

In David Mamet's play, *"Glenglarry Glen Ross"* about the brutal and humiliating lives of real estate salesmen, one of the salesmen (played by Al Pacino in the movie version) philosophises with a potentially gullible client and questions what life is all about:

> "It's looking forward to it's looking back.
> And that's our life. That's it. Where is the moment?"
>
> David Mamet (1992)

It follows from all this that the purpose and meaning of our lives cannot lie in its duration. Life is not a game of musical chairs in which the winner is the last man sitting. The triumphs of healthcare technology, and even of our cosmetic surgeons, will not forever stave off our appointment with death so uniquely captured by Sommerset Maugham in his play *"Sheppey"* [1933] in which a servant is startled by seeing the incarnation of death in the Baghdad market. In fear and in order to avoid his fate, the servant rides as fast as he can to the city of Samarra. But it turns out that it was in Samarra that very night that death had an appointment with him.

If the meaning of life and its fulfilment cannot be arrived at through duration and longevity can we find it in its antithesis? That is can meaning be found in presentism or in the present moment?

Mihaly Csikszentmihalyi describes a state of mind which he refers to as being "in the flow" and which has the following features:

1. A completely involved and focused concentration.
2. A sense of ecstasy that is of being outside of everyday reality.
3. A great inner clarity.
4. A sense of serenity, without worries about the self, a feeling of going beyond the boundaries of the ego.

5. The loss of the experience of time passing with the intense focus being on the present.

In *"Sixth Sense"* Csikszentmihalyi defines flow as the experience of optimal fulfilment and engagement. Flow can be achieved in creative arts, sports, work, or in spiritual practice. For Csikszentmihalyi, flow involves going beyond one's self, becoming immersed in something greater than one's own self. Csikszentmihalyi observed that students at the Chicago Art Institute seemed to become totally absorbed when they started to paint. They did not seem to notice anything. They appeared to be in a state of complete involvement. He surveyed chess players, mountain climbers, musicians, athletes and they all described the same type of experience: intense concentration and a loss of awareness of day to day concerns and the loss of awareness of the self. This feeling was like that of being carried by a current of water, a spontaneous, effortless "flow". Flow includes a loss of consciousness of time and a lack of the need to be in control. Flow experiences are the most memorable and the most intensely pleasurable. Striving for flow may be what gives meaning and significance to human life. People are most happy when they are in a state of flow, which is a state of total engagement with the activity at hand. Ordinary concerns about time, hunger, and self seem to melt away.

However I consider flow experiences to be instinctually neutral. That is to say that they can occur equally under life-destroying and life-affirming circumstances. They can be experienced both when the ego is being driven by the death instinct as much as by the life instinct. For example participation in a military battle induces an intense focus, engagement, exhilaration, and loss of time sense. Survivors of car accidents also describe a unique sharpening of attention and a perception of time slowing down. These may be flow experiences but not ones that we seek out; they are events in which people may die.

We will return to these ideas when we consider Edward Tronick's article on dyadically expanded states of consciousness, Ethel Spector Person's ideas about merger and Diana Fosha's concept of the "core self". But first I want to turn to another formulation of the problem of life's duration. The converse of duration is transience and it is about transience that Sigmund Freud wrote an appealing article in 1915. Entitled "On Transience" (Verganglichkeit), Freud describes going for a summer walk with two friends, one of whom was a famous poet. The poet admired the natural beauty of the surroundings but was troubled that all this beauty would be extinguished when winter came. A similar fate awaits all human beauty. Freud disagreed with his friend. He expressed the view that the transience of what is beautiful does not involve any loss in its worth, quite the contrary; limits imposed by transience raise the value of the enjoyment, just as scarcity of commodities raises their value in the market. "A flower that blossoms only for a single night does not seem to us on that account less lovely" (Freud, 1915b, p. 306). Individual beauty, works of art or intellectual achievements do not lose their worth because of their transient limits in time. Freud is making the case that the value or worth of certain sensory experiences is not dependent on their duration, in fact they have eternal value, despite or even because of their short duration.

The neurobiological basis of the experience of time

Humans and other mammals follow internal cycles and rhythms. Circadian rhythms refer to biological periods that have time frames close to the 24-hour day-night cycle. These endogenous rhythms can be entrained by the external day/night cycles but have their own independent origin in mammals including humans. The circadian rhythms are under the control of an internal "clock" which is located in the suprachiasmatic nucleus of the hypothalamus. The body's circadian clock coordinates the timing of the expression of genes within cells.

Several areas of the brain are involved in different aspects of time perception: the cerebellum; the basal ganglia; the inferior parietal lobes; the prefrontal cortex and the anterior cingulate gyrus. The cerebellum is involved in the coordination of movement which occurs within very short time intervals. The basal ganglia are active during tasks involving discrimination of time and discrimination of rhythms. The neurotransmitter dopamine is found in these brain areas and neurobiologically the flow experience may correlate with elevated and sustained levels of dopamine.

The unconscious and time

I want to turn now to a very original and elegant consideration of time published by the Boston psychiatrist, James Mann in his formative work *"Time-Limited Psychotherapy"* (1973). Mann refers to the time that we experience as "existential time". He quotes Thomas Wolfe: "Each moment is the fruit of 40,000 years. The minute-winning days, like flies, buzz home to death, and every moment is a window in all time" (Mann, 1973, p. 3).

I am drawing attention to Mann's work as it is not often studied nowadays and is less well known to the new generations of psychotherapists and psychiatrists. Yet this short book is of great importance in the ever-evolving field of short-term dynamic psychotherapy which has diverged into several currents over the past four decades. More importantly, in the present context, Mann's views are of great pertinence to the subject of this chapter. Mann comments that psychological time, unlike time that is measured by the clock, can expand or constrict in accordance with a number of factors including mood and interpersonal activity. In the unconscious, there is no awareness or experience of the passage of time. There is also a sense of timelessness in the world of children and we all recognize that time seems to speed up as we age. Time does not exist in dreams or daydreams yet when we have to confront the reality of the world around us, the sense of passing time is omnipresent. The awareness of time forces us to recognize our mortality; forces us to recognize that we all have limited time. If we can escape from the awareness of time, we can escape from the awareness of the inevitability of our deaths. Conversely, our consciousness of passing time forces us to acknowledge this actuality.

With advances in technology, rapid transportation by air, instantaneous communications by telephone and internet our sense of time and the demands of time have accelerated. We yearn for the childhood experience of timelessness. That sense of timelessness is destroyed when the infant begins to separate from the mother. To become aware of separation and reunion, it is necessary to appreciate that there is an interval of time between these two events. Separation indicates that the period of the relationship has come to an end. It reminds us that time is marching on towards that final separation which is death. Thus there is unconsciously a link between separation, time sense and the existential awareness of death. The old French proverb: "Partir c'est mourir un peu", to separate is to die a little, is true at a number of levels. Separation carries within it the implication of limited time, the implication of ultimate death.

Marie Bonaparte, a colleague and acolyte of Sigmund Freud, in an enthralling paper *"Time and the Unconscious"* which appeared in the International Journal of Psychoanalysis (1940), notes that in childhood we are not troubled by the idea of time. Young children do not seem to have an awareness of time and live in an enchanted period that is not regulated by the oppressiveness of the clock. For a child there is a sense of infinite duration. In contrast, in adult life, our days are organized in reference to our watches: a time for rising, a time for eating, a time for starting work, a time for finishing work, a time for going to sleep. There is no antidote to the passage of time and indeed the older we get, the more quickly time appears to pass. The awareness of time seems to be embedded in our higher brain functioning. Freud had long held that the unconscious is timeless; there is no sense of the passage of time in the unconscious realms of dreams and daydreams. The consciousness of time brings with it the consciousness of the journey towards death. Time thus contains within it the feeling of human horror. Time in Bonaparte's words "Takes away all that we love or regret ... ". It is within the cradle of time that we are born and acquire our existence but it is also in the cradle of time that we grow old and die losing all that we have had. Bonaparte refers to Chronus, the Greek god, who gives birth to his children but later devours them. Time has creative and destructive components.

In the context of what Mann and Bonaparte have written, it is interesting to note that we use the term "termination" both to refer to our own death and also to the end stages of psychotherapy. This reaffirms the intimate link between the limits of time, in this case in the therapy process, and the awareness of our own mortality.

Bonaparte says that within our deep unconscious, we have a profound desire to live and to escape from the fatal destructive effects of the passage of time. She identifies three states of human experience where there is a recovery of the sense of timelessness: intoxication with certain forms of drugs; mystical meditation and states of love.

Bonaparte's observations are evident in our own time with the widespread abuse of mind-altering substances. This correlates with the desire to escape from the confines of everyday life. Drugs of addiction produce a loss of awareness of reality and a diversion from life's inexorable constraints. Meditation has also become very popular with the application of "Mindfulness" in Psychotherapy. Related interests in expanding consciousness arise in the study of

Buddhism and Kabala. Bonaparte elaborates on her third category, states of love:

> " ... for the aim of the sexual act must be to attain through and beyond the ephemeral individual the substance of life that is in a sense immortal ... But it is the intoxication inherent in love, irrespective of its procreative functions, which renders its pursuit so compelling." (1940).

For the man or woman in love the experience feels eternal. Bonaparte adds: "This is why every lover swears eternal love." I would add one further category and that is Art. Art in its many forms, painting, cinema and music also evoke within us a sense of the timeless and universal in human experience; for but a brief moment it can lift us out of the daily grind.

Finally, Bonaparte raises the question as to whether time is something that really exists external to man, or whether it is a cognitive framework that is imposed upon external reality by our brains. In other words, is time a purely subjective phenomenon or is it something that exists in the real world of physical space and matter? Is time determined by the planetary motions, and the sequences of seasons, days, and nights? Or is time awareness merely the expression of our own inner biological clocks, orchestrated by the suprachiasmatic nucleus of the hypothalamus?

Killing time

Everybody is rushing to somewhere: cars on the highways; people running for the train; rushing to the airport; rushing to get to one place and then rushing to leave. Everyone is propelled into their headlong pursuits of getting through the day. There are deadlines to meet, there are children to be picked up, and there are appointments to be kept.

Timesaving technologies, computers, automobiles, airplanes, cell phones have not allowed us to do things at a more leisurely pace rather they have led to the expectations of doing more in less time; and as more things are packed into each unit of time, the perception of time becomes sped up and we wonder where the weeks and then where the years have gone. This is a process of alienation. We have become detached and defended against that which makes us truly human. Our modern techno culture is at variance with our ancestral hard wiring. We are constantly in an arousal mode of the sympathetic nervous system; our adrenaline is continuously at a high pitch. Our actions are accelerated and our interactions abbreviated. In this repetitious race, we all spend much of our lives disconnected from ourselves and disconnected from the people around us. Our technology while generating speed, distances us from human encounter. While driving on the roads we are separated from other drivers and pedestrians by a steel and glass container, the automobile. We might as well be under Sylvia Plath's "bell-jar". We are detached from other humans around us by distance and materiel. We are deprived of proximity and the sensations of touch and gesture.

While travelling on the subway I observed three young teenagers. One was wearing headphones and reading, the other two were listening to music on an i-pod. One of these was also playing an electronic game on a cell phone. Presumably three friends, but not interacting, not communicating, each in an electronic reverie.

The elevator is another convenience for the movement of people and another venue for detachment and disconnection. People are forced into uncomfortable proximity by the small size of the elevator compartment. Yet in our culture, it is rare for any of the individuals on board to acknowledge each other or to strike up a conversation. Each stands as far from the other as possible and withdraws into their own thoughts and concerns. The proximity leads to tension; the invasion of personal space is defended against by individual retreat into private fantasy and contemplation.

Where is everybody rushing to? Where are they trying to get to? What drives us forward? On the surface, it appears we are all striving to meet our basic needs at the lower levels of the Maslow hierarchy; the effort to maintain survival to provide shelter and nurture for ourselves and for our kin; the drive to avoid pain and starvation; the drive to protect our children and to ensure that they grow up in safety. Hunting and gathering are no longer modes to achieve these objectives in our society. We exist within a complex socioeconomic system, a system that requires years of preparation (education), effort and sacrifice if one is to achieve success. Long hours of work are required if one is to have not just the basic means for survival but also in order to enjoy the benefits of a fashionable home or automobile; to be able to travel and avail of entertainments.

Ironically, there is a strange converse behaviour that we all seem to indulge in every so often. This phenomenon is called "killing time". You will see people in the airports killing time waiting for their flights, people who are early for their appointments or trying to get through the weekend.

To help us kill time, we have evolved a complex array of entertainments. The French word is more evocative: "divertissements", activities that "divert" us from being left alone with our own thoughts and feelings. There is television with its mindless and time-filling talk shows and sitcoms. There are 'Gameboys' and card games, slot machines and roulette wheels. These pastimes fight off the feelings of boredom, unease and ennui that emerge in the intervals between our rushing to nowhere.

What is the connection between these two apparently antithetical pursuits: rushing to nowhere and the killing of time. The common denominator is that they both represent alienations from our authentic inner feelings and human purpose. In both states the perception of reality is diminished and lost in a haze of mental distraction and perceptual cloudiness. In the case of rushing to nowhere, our perception of time is accelerated. We have exceeded the optimal in terms of our physiology. We have acquired technology to allow this acceleration. Firstly the automobile, then the computer, the airplane, the Internet, the cell phone. We are travelling at speeds beyond that for which our neuroanatomy evolved. Multitasking requires us to be able to focus at multiple levels simultaneously.

The normal speed of action and interaction reflects the end point of millions of years of evolution and is perfectly evolved to facilitate human fulfilment that is free from the forces of alienation.

This is not to say that there are not periods of escape from rushing or killing time. Vacations to warmer lands where life is slower, allow us to reset our internal clocks in response to the splash of the waves breaking on the white sand. Or treks in the snow where the body is fully in touch with the elemental forces of nature, where the cold is bracing and mind clearing and there is a vivid sense of the surroundings. Such escapes for most of us are few and far between; for some they are never attainable. When they occur, they only serve as a contrast to the day-to-day alienation and dehumanizing currents within which we fight to avoid complete submersion.

In this chapter I have demonstrated the proposition that time is relative; that acceleration of time is associated with alienation; and that expansion of time is associated with authentic human experience. I will return to these themes of timelessness and eternity in chapter eleven when I will respond to the question posed at the beginning of this book about the meaning of our lives.

CHAPTER TEN

Meaning

Proposition #10 The need for meaning is a fundamental
property of human nature

The question of the meaning of life has preoccupied humans
since the evolution of the faculty of consciousness. For us the
span from birth to death is a mere 50 to 80 years, an infini-
tesimal amount in the context of a universe, billions of years old.
What then is to be made of the purpose of human life over this brief
time?

The search for meaning in life is important to those who already
have their basic survival needs satisfied. For those groups of people
still struggling to obtain the basic necessities of life, safety, shelter,
food and sustenance, the search for meaning may be displaced by
the urgent demands of survival. For people in developed Western
societies who take many of these survival basics for granted, there
may arise a troublesome apprehension as to the purpose and meaning of life. We thirst to know if we are the product of some universal
divine plan or the random concatenation of molecules that led to
the formation of DNA. Is the purpose of life to transcend the mate-

rial world in order to achieve moral or idealistic purity? If so, to paraphrase Schopenhauer, the divine plan (now often referred to as "intelligent design") appears to have gone badly astray based on the observable results!

Conversely, is all appeal to a higher power merely an illusion as Freud so eloquently argued. If then we arrive here by random forces are we merely then vehicles of the "selfish gene", the DNA that strives inexorably to replicate itself, casting aside the bodily shell as it passes from one generation to the next.

If we are random products, if there is no supernatural or divine plan or purpose, are we then left to choose our own purpose as the existentialists contend? There is no "essence" before "existence". The world is random, probabilistic, meaningless and absurd; but seeing that we are here anyway, we might as well make the best of it and define our own purposes and meaning.

There are those who seek meaning and purpose in the pursuit of pleasure, the gratification of bodily desires, the hunt for sexual fulfilment and material luxury. Or the indulgence of the senses of taste, smell, hearing, vision and touch, the visual arts, music. The pursuit of pleasure and the perfection of the gastronomic palate was practiced by the followers of Epicurus over 2000 years ago and is glaringly evident in our own day.

Or is life about the renunciation of the animal and aesthetic impulses? Does it call for spiritual transcendence as seen, for example, in Buddhist or Christian monks?

If we are born without purpose, without signposts, how then can we ascertain the path that man should take? One is forced to return to Freud as one of the few authorities who has attempted to construct a comprehensive and wide-ranging model of human psychology. Freud based his theories on naturalistic observation, careful clinical scrutiny and self-reflection. For Freud, the essence of the dilemma is to be found in the struggle between the life instincts and the death instincts: between Eros and Thanatos. In Freud's schema, man is driven by the pleasure principle; the imperative to reduce feelings of "unpleasure" and tension. But this unbridled drive cannot be given free reign because it comes into conflict with the rest of society and must therefore be governed by the "reality principle". Compromises must be made through the mediation of the "ego" between the instinctual pressures of the "id" and the countervailing censures of the internalized parental and societal prohibitions, the "superego". For Freud, civilization requires the renunciation and repression of large quantities of these drives. Family structures and the institution of monogamy are required for the orderly pursuit of economic activity, the division of labour, reproduction and the upbringing of children. Without this compromise, the free expression of the instincts would lead to disorganization, patricide and chaos. Instead the instinctual energy is channelled ("sublimated") into the business of society: work, education and economic activity.

Marcuse (1955), has written about the repressive "desublimation" of the instincts. Superficially in modern technological society, there appears to be a lifting of the repression and suppression of instinctual gratification. This is manifest in the more open acknowledgment and display of human sexuality in every day life: in dress, in art, in the media and on the internet and in the proliferation of pornography and sexually charged advertising. These appear to permit some gratification of sexual drives but on closer scrutiny it is seen that this gratification is hijacked in the interests of commercialism and consumption. The gratification is never integral or complete but is rather frustrated and partial producing an addictive craving for more. Such a state is perfectly suited to the commercial enterprise of instinct driven consumption. So Western society, which on the surface may look like it has evolved towards greater and more natural expression of sexuality, in fact represents a more insidious and subtle manipulation of the instincts in the pursuit of profit. Rather than giving free natural and wholesome expression to our inner drives, these have been subverted in the race for profitability and consumption.

Let us now turn to an entirely different view of the problem of meaning. This view postulates that the concept of man as a unique and individual agent bounded by his bodily presence is in fact an illusion. Einstein has put this well, as has the popular author and public speaker Deepak Chopra. This point of view can be simply summarised in the words of the famous musical "Hair" which premiered in the 60's. In one of its songs it states that we are all "stardust". Ultimately we all came from the atoms that emerged from the big bang and that the boundaries between us and our environment are an artificial outcome of our consciousness. Consequently, meaning cannot be found in the life of the individual or society but can only be found in the broader domains of the planet and the universe.

Humans are unique among species in that we possess the capacity for self consciousness. This includes a consciousness of our bodies; we have a sense of where are bodies are located in space; we have an internal schema of our own anatomy that constitutes a primitive sense of self. This capability for body awareness may be shared by other higher mammals, such as primates and dolphins (Kirkaldie T.K., & Kitchener P.D. 2007). This faculty may be an emergent property that depends on the size of the neocortex. Humans have the largest neocortex. Body awareness arises from multiple feedback from visual, tactile and positional sensory information. This explains the phantom limb phenomenon, after amputation. In this the patient continues to feel the presence of the missing limb. The representation of the limb persists in the brain/cerebral cortex and the individual continues to experience pain as if it were coming from the now severed limb (Critchley 1979). Based on clinical neurological observations in those with brain injuries and strokes, it is believed that corporeal awareness resides in the non-dominant parietal lobe of the brain.

It is possible to undergo a temporary loss of our corporeal awareness. We feel as if we are looking down upon our selves from above or at a distance. This is referred to as "depersonalization" and can occur in a variety of psychiatric conditions but most commonly during periods of heightened anxiety. Critchley (1979) cites an example of a woman who describes the orgasmic experience as including the sense of the body dissolving. But humans have in addition another level of awareness: the awareness of self. We are aware of ourselves as agents of action, feeling, emotion and thought. It is this level of awareness that gives rise to the quest for meaning.

Victor Frankl (2004), a survivor of the Nazi concentration camps, contends that the search for meaning is the primary motivating force in man.

Over many millennia religious belief has provided mankind with meaning and purpose. Freud in "The Future of an Illusion" argued that religion grew out of man's feelings of helplessness in the face of the terrors of nature, the inevitability of death, and because of the need for instinctual repression in the conduct of social life and civilization. Freud found a parallel between the ceremonies and rituals of religion and the compulsive behaviours seen in individuals with obsessive neurosis. He described religion as a universal obsessive neurosis. Both display belief in magical thinking, that is that thoughts and wishes can affect things in the real world without action. Such illusions of a benevolent father figure in the form of gods or God, act as an anodyne to man's deep-rooted existential fears. Religion provides an illusory explanation of the mysteries of life and the universe. In *"Civilizations and It's Discontents"* Freud says

> "The whole thing is so patently infantile, so incongruous with reality, that ... it is painful to think that the great majority of mortals will never be able to rise above this view of life" (Freud, 1930a, p. 74).

Religions are "mass delusions". He adds: "needless to say, no one who shares a delusion recognizes it as such" (Freud, 1930a, p. 81).

Freud in the same work postulated that man is driven by "the pleasure principle" whose purpose and object is to eliminate pain and discomfort and to strive for the experiences of intense pleasure. Happiness results from the satisfaction of inner drives but such satisfaction is transitory. Rather without meaning we feel empty. There is no point to life; nothing matters and there is no deterrent to suicide. Indeed this is the potency of Hamlet's universally recognized question "To be or not to be?".

For Jean Paul Sartre the French philosopher and the other existentialists there is no meaning. Life and death are random accidents of nature. There is no meaning to life and no meaning to death. Existence is absurd. This reality leads us to despair. Sartre wrote in his play *"The Flies"*, that "Human life begins on the far side of despair" (Sartre, 1989, p. 81). It is only by recognizing that there is no pre-ordained meaning to life that we can be "authentic". Then we can accept that we must invent our own meaning and then commit ourselves to it. Those who are unable to take this leap of engagement may end up submitting slavishly to a totalitarian ideology in which all answers and meaning are provided by the leader. This was most evident in wartime Germany and in China in the time of Mao.

The Irish poet, W.B. Yeats had inscribed on his tombstone in County Sligo:

> "Cast a cold eye on life and death
> Horsemen pass by"

Yeats meant by these words that there is no value in contemplating life or death and he instructs the passing rider and us to carry on with our actions. Life and death have no meaning; it is the journey that counts. For Sartre man must choose his meaning by engaging with life through action and making a commitment.

Shakespeare captures the futility of life in *"Macbeth"*:

> "To-morrow, and to-morrow, and to-morrow,
> Creeps in this petty pace from day to day,
> To the last syllable of recorded time;
> And all our yesterdays have lighted fools
> The way to dusty death. Out, out, brief candle!
> Life's but a walking shadow; a poor player,
> That struts and frets his hour upon the stage,
> And then is heard no more: it is a tale
> Told by an idiot, full of sound and fury,
> Signifying nothing." *Macbeth* (V, v, 19)

Yet we continue to seek meaning in different ways. One of the commonest is to adopt a cause, pursuing a political or ideological dream. By belonging to a political movement one's identity becomes merged with the group. Meaning and purpose are derived from the aims of the political party. Taking up a career dedicated to the helping of others such as medicine or nursing is another source of a meaningful life. In a related theme there is a Jewish tradition that the world is broken, that something went wrong during the process of earthly creation and that man's purpose and meaning is to heal the world which in Hebrew is rendered as "tikkun olam".

Meaning may be sought through creativity and generativity, giving birth to children and ensuring their welfare, growth and success. The creation of works of art and things of beauty is another vehicle for this.

Self-actualization is the source of meaning described by Abraham Maslow (see introduction). The ultimate goal here is to reach the highest level of expression of one's inner self.

Some believe that the direct pursuit of meaning is futile. For them meaning is a by-product of striving in life. Action in life is the essential precursor.

The existentialists champion the acceptance of despair and recommend that we look into its dark abyss. We must create our own meaning and indeed we are free to choose to do so.

Freud's response to this question was beguilingly simple: the purpose of life is "to love and to work". To love requires one to pass through the appropriate developmental and social milestones in order to be able to establish an attachment with another person. To work also requires the attainment of certain capacities within a social context in order to be productive.

Meaning in love and loss

There is a striking contrast between the Freudian and Sartrean views. For Freud, man's meaning is derivative of his inborn drives that achieve expression in his daily pursuits and relations. For Sartre there is no inner meaning that seeks its own expression. There is no preordained "essence" to use his term. Rather we must construct our own meaning. These opposing conceptions are a version of the historic antagonism between the proponents of determinism and free will. Freud is a biological determinist. Sartre is an expositor of freedom and choice.

One of the propositions of this book is that the meaning of our lives can be derived from our unique biological inheritance. Its origins are in the imperative to attach. As we saw in the Chapter Three, our sense of identity and self develops out of our attachment experiences. But along the way we are forced by the social and physical environment to build walls of defences to prevent the annihilation of the self from external dangers. This may lead to the construction of a "false self", a term coined by Donald Winnicott or to an "inauthentic self", in Sartre's terms. When we are in thrall to a false self, we feel detached from life; there is a lack of vigour and a lack of vividness in perceptions. Above all there is sense of meaninglessness and emptiness. Could it be that within the dichotomy between a true and a false self, lies a clue to the enigma of human meaning?

CHAPTER ELEVEN

The love connection

Proposition #11 The primary drive to attach gives rise to the strongest sense of meaning in human interaction.

L ove is a search for completion. In the Symposium Plato describes humans as having eight limbs, two faces and two sets of genitals. Because of human arrogance, Zeus cut the humans in half and scattered the halves in opposite directions. Humans are always searching for their complementary half. Eros (love) is the desire to become one again, to become whole. In accounts of love, as we have seen, the theme of union and merger is a recurrent one. This is evident in great art such as Munch's *"The Kiss"* (Figure 2) and in poetry and song:

> "When love, with one another so
> Interinanimates two souls,
> That abler soul, which thence doth flow,
> Defects of loneliness controls".

John Donne. The Ecstasy

For Donne loneliness is overcome when two souls unite in a new "abler soul".

And again themes of union:

> "But we will have a way more liberal
> Than changing hearts, to join them; so we shall
> Be one, and one another's all".

John Donne. *Lover's Infiniteness*

Ethel Person (2007) states "passionate love tends to overcome the pain of separation, separateness and the felt inadequacies of the solitary self, through merger with the Other". Pearson writes that although lovers may strive for complete merger, this cannot take place, but there are "ecstatic moments of merger" which are experienced as "epiphanies". During these times, there is a loss or partial loss of ego boundaries which is accompanied by a sense of "timelessness, bliss and transcendence" (page 103–4). I would add to her formulation the following question: Is this the return to the original dyadic state between mother and infant, with its sense of satiety and complete fulfilment?

In merger, much of the current "self" dissolves away and becomes coextensive with the self of the other. For Person, the lovers regain "a primordial tensionless state of consciousness".

This love connection can be seen as crossing the existential abyss of aloneness. If we look again at Edvard Munch's portrait of *"The Young Woman on the Shore"* (Figure 3), we see the back of a young woman with blonde hair, dressed in white, looking out towards looking out towards the vast horizon. The painting is stark and devoid of detail. It creates a sense of being alone in a vast universe. Such a state of aloneness can evoke the terror of the scream in Munch's more famous painting. It is reminiscent of the separation of the infant from its mother. This incites terror because with it comes the risk of death by starvation or as the victim of predators.

Esther Perel puts it clearly when she says that such a moment "re-enacts that most prime primitive form of early fusion—the merging of bodies, the nipple that fills our entire mouth and leaves us completely satiated" (Perel, 2006, p. 180). However, she cautions that there are two poles within love: "surrender" and "autonomy". She states that too much merging obliterates the separateness of the two individuals.

When two people are fused there is no process of connection to navigate. For Perel, separateness is a precondition for connection which she calls "the essential paradox of intimacy and sex" (2006, p. 25).

Person on the same theme points out that each individual must have enough faith in their own autonomy in order to be able to let go and give into the sense of merger. "One finds oneself only by losing oneself" (Person, 2007, p. 105).

For some the merged state may carry with it the risk of engulfment. This is particularly true of the borderline personality who oscillates between fears of abandonment and fears of engulfment. But, for the well adjusted the state of merger brings with it great exhilaration, pleasure and meaning. At such times the ego defences are suspended; elements of "the false self" drop away exposing "the core self" and it is in the discovery and re-experiencing of the "core self" that a true state of liberation is found.

It follows from this line of reasoning that we can only penetrate to our "core selves" when we are in a certain type of relation to the other.

Schizoid adaptation

The greatest fear of engulfment is seen in the schizoid personality disorder. These individuals appear aloof and detached from social relationships; they have a restricted range of emotions. They choose solitary activities and appear to have no interest in sexual relationships. They lack close friends and are affectively flat. Inwardly they are exquisitely sensitive. Their self-representation is fragmented. They lack a clear sense of who they are, rather experiencing a confusing mix of thoughts, urges and feelings. Their inner needs are so vast that they are fearful of yielding to them. They are terrified of being overwhelmed and engulfed by the other in the relationship. They are afraid of being devoured, smothered and consumed. They live in constant dread of annihilation. A loving relationship would result in the loss of one's self. The schizoid retreats from all relationships because they are inherently dangerous and potentially annihilating. He withdraws from social interactions and engages in solitary and isolated pursuits.

The false self

Donald Winnicott, the British paediatrician and psychoanalyst, introduced the concept of the "false self". The mother or mother figure must provide a "good enough" environment. A "good enough mother" cannot and does not meet perfectly all of the infant's needs; there is inevitably some deprivations and lack of gratification. This ensures an appropriately balanced development. The good enough environment must provide adequate protection and nurturance but must also provide some awareness that all needs cannot always be met in the real world. If the mother figure is not able to provide such an environment the infant is unable to express its own spontaneous feelings and desires. Instead a set of behaviours and attitudes develop in order to appease the unsustaining mother. The infant develops a false self that reacts in compliance to the mother's demands. The true self is hidden and suppressed and cannot be given spontaneous expression because of the hostile environment. The true feelings of authenticity and genuineness are buried under the gestures, behaviour, and defences of the false self.

Winnicott states that "only the True Self can be creative and only the True Self can feel real." (Winnicott, 1965, p. 146). The false self is accompanied by a sense of unreality and futility.

The core self

Diana Fosha (2005) arrives at a similar destination but via a different route: the route is a school of dynamic psychotherapy: Accelerated Experiential Dynamic Psychotherapy. She elaborates her view in her 2005 article identifying three states that are evident in therapy. Firstly there is a state of defence at the beginning of therapy during which the patient keeps his most painful feelings and wishes in abeyance. Secondly there is a state of core affect that emerges when the defences are challenged in therapy. When the defences are confronted, the patient is able to feel the full "visceral experience" of core affects. This involves dealing with feelings of anxiety, shame and fear. There has been a breakthrough to the core affects which are processed in the right brain. This is analogous to Davanloo's (1990) method of "unlocking the unconscious". Previously, buried feelings, thoughts and memories can now be accessed through the experience and validation of these affects. In therapy, in the present moment, the individual "feels in deep contact with the truth of his own subjective experience and has a heightened sense of authenticity and vitality ... clarity and well being predominate". This third state is the experience of the real authentic core self. Sensation is heightened and images are more vivid. The relationship is deep and clear. Defensiveness has evaporated and there is a sense of calm and clarity. The "false self" is penetrated to uncover the true self.

This state is further characterised by "relaxation, ease, clarity and wellbeing". Here again deep connects with deep but this time it is through the vehicle of the psychotherapeutic dyad. What are the implications of this for the relationship between the mother and infant, the mother-infant dyad? For that we turn to Edward Tronick.

The dyadic expanded state of consciousness

Edward Tronick (1998) proposes in his article, "*Dyadically Expanded States of Consciousness and the Process of Therapeutic Change*", that the mutual regulation of affect that occurs between infant and mother leads to an expanded state of consciousness. This "dyadic system contains more information, is more complex and coherent" than either the infant or mother's state of consciousness alone. Both the infant's and mother's experience of consciousness conflates, each incorporating elements of the other, "in a new and more coherent form". Tronick states that this is consonant with the first principle of systems theory, which is that open systems incorporate and integrate increasing amounts of information into more complex but more coherent states. This is an expansion of consciousness and subjectively may be accompanied by a feeling of fulfilment and discovery.

Tronick views this process as a model for psychotherapeutic change which also occurs in an "asymmetrical" relationship. As we have seen in Chapter One above (Attachment), there is a mutual interplay between mother and infant that leads to a synchrony. This synchrony is mediated by the infant's emotional states, body rhythms, facial expressions and vocalizations. Tronick believes that such mutual attunement also occurs in psychotherapy and results in the organization of a dyadic system that has increasing levels of complexity and coherence. He says that mutual regulation of social interactions "requires a mutual mapping of elements of each partners state of consciousness into the other partners brain". In therapy the patient experiences a "reintegration and reconfiguring" of existing states of consciousness: a qualitatively new and unique expansion of consciousness.

Neurobiological support for these ideas is given by the recent discovery of "mirror neurons" Gallese (2007). We gain an experiential understanding of others by modelling their behaviours in our own brains so that we feel what they feel. When the mirror neurons are activated they give the observer the same bodily sensations and emotions that are experienced by the person who is being observed.

Mirror neurons were first discovered in monkeys. A specific group of neurons will fire when a monkey breaks a peanut. What is striking is that when one monkey observes another monkey breaking a peanut or hears the sound of a peanut being broken, there is activation of the corresponding neurons within the observing monkey. Functional magnetic resonant imaging (fMRI) studies have identified mirror neurons in the inferior frontal cortex and in parts of the inferior parietal lobule (Uddin 2007). There are at least two neural networks in the brain that represent self and others. Self and other may be "two sides of the same coin whether their physical interactions or their most internal mental processes are examined".

Themes of merger, fusion, and symbiosis recur both in popular culture as well as in psychoanalytic theory. But there is another very powerful motif: reference to the infinite, the eternal, the timeless. I am not referring here to anything that might be construed as "spiritual" or "transcendent" in a religious or supernatural sense. I wish to stay very much within the realm of human that is secular experience and discourse.

There is a tradition in English literature of the Romantic period (1798–1832) that man is driven by a quest for the *infinite*. This is illustrated dramatically in John Keats' poem about the search for immortal love, Endymion:

> "… But there are
> Richer entanglements, enthralments far
> More self-destroying, leading, by degrees,
> To the chief intensity: the crown of these
> Is made of love and friendship, and sits high
> Upon the forehead of humanity".

Keats is claiming that through the loss of self we reach the crowning intensity of human experience in love and friendship. As to the highest of these, he asserts:

> "and that is love: its influence,
> Thrown in our eyes, genders a novel sense,
> At which we start and fret; till in the end,
> Melting into its radiance, we blend,
> Mingle, and so become a part of it,—"

And it is as a result of this merging, or in Keats' word "melting", that we attain a sense beyond the limits of experienced solace and time.

> "Now, if this earthly love has power to make
> Men's being mortal, immortal; to shake
> Ambition from their memories, and brim
> Their measure of content; what merest whim,
> Seems all this poor endeavour after fame,
> To one, who keeps within his steadfast aim
> A love immortal, an immortal too.
>
> John Keats. *Endymion* (1817)

I am quoting from Keats as a poetic endorsement of one of my major themes: that it is in the dissolution of certain aspects of the self, I would say the relinquishing of maladaptive defences and the false self, that one acquires an experience that is not bounded by our usual experiences of psychological time and space. The same themes of eternal love and timelessness are evident in a myriad of popular songs of our own day; references to moments that appear to stretch out; of feelings that seem as if they will last forever. One only has to turn on the radio or connect to iTunes to confirm the universality of these extraordinary human experiences.

Martin Buber

> "The world is twofold for man ..., In accordance with his twofold attitude" (Buber, 1970, p. 53).

Buber puts forth that man can adapt one of two attitudes in his relations to the world around him: "I-it" and "I-you". Buber's philosophy is one of encounter, of dialogue.

The first attitude, I-it consists of relating to objects or other people as "things" to objectify them, to do things to them, to use them or to "experience them" as objects. "I cannot be defined in isolation, the I is determined by which of the two attitudes is currently in play". This concept has parallels with the psychoanalytic concept of relating to "a part object".

The "I-you" is a direct encounter "spoken only with ones whole being". Such "a concentration and fusion into a whole being, can never be accomplished by me, can never be accomplished without me. I require a you to become: becoming I, I say you". (Buber, 1970, p. 62).

For Buber love is not a feeling, rather feelings accompany "the metaphysical and metapsychical fact of love, but they do not constitute it:" (Buber, 1970, p. 66). One has feelings when love "occurs". The "you" is not merely an object of ones feelings of love; love is what occurs "between I and you".

The true encounter occurs fully in the present, in a spaceless and timeless present. It is between one whole human being and another whole human being, not the individual as considered as an aggregate of parts and characteristics. Man is defined by this dialogue. The dyad, man in relation, is his essence. Not the monologue of analysis where man is seen from the perspective of psychology, sociology, physiology, etc., A thing of multiple elements and parts.

But is Buber correct when he says that love is not a feeling but is the relation, the encounter? One can see the contrast with current views regarding relationships which "objectify women" for example where the relationship is of one person acting on the other or using the other for gratification. This is a form of "I-It" relationship and not a genuine encounter.

But does the view that love is not a feeling jibe with our neurobiological understanding that attachment and the feeling of romantic love are very much tied up to neurocircuits and in particular to the dopamine reward system and the opioid receptors?

Contrast Buber's views with those of psychoanalysis where love seems to be a manifestation of an epic search, a craving for the reestablishment of the primary relationship with the primary love object. The relationship then is not one of a pure encounter but one that is contaminated by the projections of each person onto the other which distorts the true reality of the other by means of the transference phenomenon. The act of loving becomes a merger, a dissolving of the ego boundaries and again may be experienced as something removed from time and space. One can again see this manifested in Munch's painting of "The Kiss" (Figure 2), of two embracing figures whose faces merge and blend into each other.

There are two very critical and emotionally acute transitions when two people are in love. These are the times of meeting and the times of departure.

The time of meeting, the re-initiation of encounter, is presaged by a heightened sense of anticipation, melancholy, excitement tinged with apprehension that the meeting may not take place. This is followed by the impact of the meeting, the collision of the encounter and the sense of fusion.

The second event is the separation, the departure which provokes all the painful feelings of loss which resonate with the earliest feelings of loss, the separation from the primary attachment figure. This is the reciprocal of merging and fusion. It is the painful confirmation of the boundaries between one and the other or in Winnicott's terms. The awareness of the self which is defined by the differentiation of "me and not me".

But then again, perhaps love resides in Winnicott's in between space; the transitional space. This clearly is not the same "between" as that of Martin Buber. The transitional space consists of the blending of inner feelings, thoughts and emotions with elements in the external world.

Regardless of which view may be closer to the truth, the Buberian or the psychoanalytic, there is a corollary to these theorems: if ultimately the essence of an authentic encounter implies and requires the loss of awareness of both time and space (or perhaps involves a state where the concepts of time and space no longer have meaning) then important experiences do not depend on location or duration. Thus, it may not matter how long an individual may live his life or where he may live it but rather whether or not he is able to enter into a true encounter even when he is on the point of his death. Even then it is possible for him to enter into a true encounter that is timeless and spaceless and therefore eternal. All that persists, all that is timeless, derives from love.

And back to the staring point of our journey in this book, Romeo and Juliet:

> "My bounty is as boundless as the sea, my love as deep; the more I give to thee, the more I have, for both are **infinite**." (emphasis added).

(Act 2, Scene 2)

Walter Kaufmann in his prologue to his translation of "I and Thou" draws a comparison between Buber's thinking and that of William Blake:

> "To see a world in a grain of sand
> and a Heaven in a wild flower
> Hold infinity in the palm of your hand
> And Eternity in an hour".

William Blake: *Auguries of Innocence*

It is my contention that it is in the dyadic encounter with the primary love object that the experience of timelessness and meaning reaches its apogee. The eternity that Blake describes in his sublime poetry is experienced in its most intense form in the primary relationship. I have adduced evidence for this from psychoanalysis, philosophy, poetry and neurobiology. It is this that is the ultimate expression of man's life-affirming drive for self-preservation and relationship. And it is this that provides us with the greatest sense of meaning and fulfilment.

"The aim of Eros is to establish unities ... the aim of Thanatos is to undo connections and so to destroy things". (Laplanche & Pontalis, 1976, p. 103). The aggressive instinct is derived from the death instinct, directed outwards. It is the conflict between the life and death instincts that lies at the centre of the human predicament. It is the struggle to suppress and neutralize the effects of the death instinct and to promote and maximize the life instinct, in the form of attachment and love that constitutes a prime element of life's meaning.

Our search for meaning stops at this point. Human meaning is to be found in the authentic dyadic encounter, which carries us subjectively beyond time and space to a rediscovery of our true selves. To permit this dyad to flourish we are forced to confront and to resist the ever-present challenge of the death instinct and its destructive materializations.

CHAPTER TWELVE

Conclusion

B ased on the arguments and propositions developed throughout this book, I can now address the questions raised in the introduction:

All of us seek to understand the meaning of life, and especially the meaning of our own lives. We struggle with the mysteries of birth and death, of love and loss. These are fundamental to our nature as human beings. But what drives us? What impels us on our daily round of tasks and relationships? What propels us forward in pursuit of what unclear purpose, what ill- defined and hazy consummation?

My conclusion is that the purpose of life is to strive for the discovery and expression of the life-affirming components of the true self. The discovery or perhaps recovery of the true self occurs in the authentic and timeless encounter between two people. It is the rediscovery of elements of the primary attachments in the joining together of two human beings. I propose to call relationships that fulfil this promise, as described in Chapter Eleven, "resonant relationships."

I will recap the development of my argument and its building blocks. I began by recounting that attachment is the pre-eminent human drive and is the matrix within which human identity is formed (Propositions #1, 2 and 3). It is through the dyadic relationship with the primary attachment figures that one's identity develops.

Proposition #1 The drive to attach is fundamental and primary to human nature.

Proposition #2 Strivings for attachment are the strongest motivators of human behaviour.

Proposition #3 Identity is formed from interpersonal interaction, and emerges from the repeated interactions with the attachment figures.

Mood regulation is strongly influenced by the dyadic relationship. Attachment is a key vehicle for the regulation of affect. When the early attachment relationships are "good enough", this provides the basis for the growth of a healthy personality (propositions 1, 2, 3, 4a, 4b, 5, 6):

Proposition #4a Mood is the bedrock of identity and the sense of self.

Proposition #4b Instability of mood gives rise to instability of the sense of Identity.

Proposition #5 Psychiatric disorders both reflect and affect the expression of love and loss.

Proposition #6 Disorders of sexual desire comprise the inability to maintain healthy attachments simultaneously with sexual intercourse.

The chapters on loss and suicide demonstrated the acute effects loss of primary attachment figures may have. Loss can unleash self-destructive forces; one extreme effect is suicide (propositions 7 and 8):

Proposition #7 The intensity of loss and grief is directly proportional to the intensity of the attachment bond and its felt component: love.

Proposition #8 The death instinct exerts its effects when attachments are lost.

The exposition on time in chapter nine sets a foundation for chapter ten which describes man's quest for meaning as a fundamental human need which can realise itself in resonant relationships that are characterised by a sense of timelessness and authenticity (propositions 9, 10, 11):

Proposition #9 Time is relative; acceleration of time is associated with alienation; expansion of time is associated with authentic human experience.

Proposition #10 The need for meaning is a fundamental property of human nature.

Proposition #11 The primary drive to attach gives rise to the strongest sense of meaning in human interaction.

Attachment glossary

Attachment: inborn program of behaviour that brings mother and child into proximity.

Distress vocalizations: the cries and sounds emitted by the infant when separated from the attachment figure.

Dyad: A two person relationship

Primary attachment figure: the person to whom the baby attaches. This is the person that cares for the infant for the major part of the time, most frequently the mother but this role may be undertaken by others. Primary attachment is analogous to "primary love object" in object relations theory.

Proximity seeking: the infant's tendency to seek closeness to the attachment figure.

Secondary attachment figure: includes others to whom the infant is in close proximity and who share in his care: the father, siblings, grandparents, schoolmates, teachers etc. These relationships supplement or mitigate the effects of the primary attachment relationship.

Separation distress: the distress experienced by the infant when separated from the attachment figure.

Neuroscience glossary

Affect: the subjective feeling part of emotion.

Amygdala: a small almond shaped structure located deep in the front part of the temporal lobe, made up of a number of nuclei. The amygdala plays important roles in the expression of aggression and fear, has an important role in memory in relation to emotionally charged events and the ability to make social interpretations of facial expressions.

Basal Ganglia: a group of neuron clusters located deep inside the cortex. They facilitate movement. Their function is impaired in Parkinson's disease.

Cerebellum: a lobular structure at the back of the brain. It is behind and below the occipital lobe and functions to coordinate movement.

Cerebral cortex: a convoluted outer layer of grey matter made up of nerve cells and their connections. This is the most recent part of the brain that achieves its most full evolution in the human. It is divided into several regions: the frontal lobe, parietal lobe, temporal lobe and the occipital lobe. The left side of the cerebral cortex is involved in logical processing such as speech and mathematics; the right side is related to global and impressionistic thinking, spatial relationships and emotions.

Cingulate gyrus: a long semicircular tract running below the main part of the cerebral cortex towards the centre of the brain. The anterior cingulate is connected to the amygdala, the posterior cingulate is connected to the hippocampus.

Hypothalamus: a group of nuclei centrally located at the front and base of the brain. It is linked to the pituitary gland and thereby links the brain to the endocrine system. The hypothalamus produces the hormones oxytocin and vasopressin, which are released directly to the posterior pituitary. The hypothalamus regulates basic drives such as appetite, thirst, and sexual arousal. This is intimately linked to the pituitary gland and the control of certain endocrine functions.

Hippocampus: part of the cortex located within the inside fold of each temporal lobe. It has a major role in memory and learning.

Limbic system: a series of circuits and nuclei in the deeper, older part of the brain that include the cingulate gyrus, the hippocampus and the amygdala. The limbic system is the source of emotion and motivation.

MRI: magnetic resonance imaging. Detects radiofrequency signals from atomic nuclei in order to produce two-dimensional detailed images of the brain. Functional MRI (fMRI) detects changes in blood flow when an area of the brain is functioning.

Mu receptor: a subtype of receptor on which opioid neurotransmitters act.

Neuron: the basic active cell unit within the brain. Neurons conduct nerve impulses from one cell to another.

Neurotransmitters: chemical agents that pass across the synapse from one neuron to another e.g. dopamine, norepinephrine, gaba.

Nucleus: a cluster of neurons.

Nucleus accumbens: a cluster of neurons in the forebrain involved in the experience of pleasure and reward. Addictive drugs such as cocaine and amphetamines increase dopamine levels in this nucleus.

Opioid neurotransmitters: a group of neurotransmitters that are related to opiate drugs like morphine.

Pituitary gland: a small pea-like structure in the centre of the skull that is a major control centre for the endocrine system. It controls the function of the thyroid gland, the adrenals and ovaries. Prolactin is released from the anterior pituitary gland.

PET: positron emission tomography detects positrons emitted from radioactive chemicals (isotopes) to yield very detailed images of brain function.

Receptor: areas on the neuron surface to which neurotransmitters bind.

Serotonin: also known as 5-HT, an important neurotransmitter involved in mood regulation.

Synapse: the tiny space between one neuron and another. Neuro-transmitters move across this gap from one neuron ending to act on the receptors of another.

Ventral Tegmental Area: located in the midbrain and connected to the nucleus accumbens and the frontal cortex by dopamine pathways. Part of the pleasure-reward circuit.

Psychoanalytic glossary

Conflict theory: Freud's theory that human behaviour is determined by inner conflicts between opposing mental forces. There is conflict between the drives of the id and the rational requirements of the ego.

Death instinct: the tendency of every living thing to return to the inorganic state.

Defences: unconscious automatic mental processes that serve to reduce anxiety in response to internal or external threats. Common defence mechanisms are sublimation, displacement, reaction formation, projection, and humour.

Drive theory: Freud's view that drives are central in human development and behaviour. The principle drives are the sexual and aggressive drives.

Ego: refers to the rational thinking part of the brain that mediates between internal drives of the id and the requirements of social reality and moral standards.

Eros: refers to the life instincts, which includes the sexual instinct and the instincts for self-preservation.

Id: refers to the unconscious instinctual drives, which include aggression and sexuality.

Instinct: an inborn striving that seeks expression such as the sexual instinct. Instincts have an inner bodily source and have an aim directed towards an object.

Internalization: the taking into the mental structure of a representation of a relationship or object.

Object: in psychoanalysis is not a thing but rather refers to another person.

Object relations theory: in contrast to drive, theory is based on the belief that relationships between people are the basic underlying processes in mental development rather than internal drives and conflicts.

Pleasure principle: an overriding principle that governs mental functioning. It postulates that mental activity is aimed at obtaining pleasure and avoiding pain.

Reality principle: the second principle governing human behaviour that must take into account external reality and the dangerous consequences of the modified expression of the pleasure principle. The reality principle is associated with the functions of the ego. The pleasure principle is associated with the demands of the id.

Superego: roughly correlates with the term conscience. It contains the internal prohibitions and moral values that are acquired in the course of development.

Brief biographical sketches of key figures

Michael Balint: (1896–1970) Hungarian analyst and one of the members of the British psychoanalytic society. Described "primary love".

Jacob Bronowski: (1908–1974) Born in Poland and educated at Cambridge where he conducted mathematical research. Held several important research and scientific advisory positions in the British Government during and after World War II. He subsequently moved to the Salk Institute for Biological Studies in La Jolla California. He wrote eloquently on the relationship between science and human values.

John Bowlby: (1907–1990) British psychoanalyst who conceptualized Attachment theory. He worked for many years at the Tavistock Clinic in London and was a member of the Medical Research Council. Author of the groundbreaking trilogy: Attachment, Separation, and Loss.

W.R.D. Fairbairn: (1889–1964) Scottish psychiatrist. A central figure in the British object relations school postulated that object seeking is the primary human drive.

Kahlil Gibran: (1883–1931) Born in Lebanon, settled in the United States. Poet, philosopher and artist.

Melanie Klein: (1882–1960) Born in Vienna, moved to London in 1926. Pioneered psychoanalytic work with children and was the key originator of object relations theory.

Margaret Mahler: (1897–1985) Born in Hungary, she moved to New York from Vienna in 1938. She established a therapeutic nursery at the Masters Children's Center in New York City. Based on her observations she conceptualized psychological development as a process of separation and individuation.

Abraham Maslow: (1908–1970) American psychologist and leader in humanistic psychology. He developed the concept of self-actualization.

Edvard Munch: (1863–1944) Considered Norway's greatest painter; lived for periods in France and Germany. He is most widely known for his haunting painting "The Scream."

Jaak Panksepp: a behavioural neuroscientist at the Department of Psychology, Bowling Green State University in Ohio. The author of the pioneering work, Affective Neuroscience (1998).

Jean-Paul Sartre: (1905–1980) French novelist, playwright and internationally renowned philosopher.

Donald Winnicott: (1897–1971) an English paediatrician and psychoanalyst. He developed the concepts of good-enough mothering, transitional object and false self.

BIBLIOGRAPHY

Abrams, M.H., Talbot, E., Smith, H., Adams, R.M., Monk, S.H., Lipking, L., Ford, G.H., Daiches, D. (1975). *The Norton Anthology of English Literature*. New York: W.W. Norton.

Akhtar, S., Kramer, S. (1996). *Intimacy and Infidelity Separation—Individuation Perspectives*. New Jersey: Jason Aronson.

Alvarez, A. (1971). *The Savage God a Study of Suicide*. London: Weidenfeld and Nickolson.

American Psychiatric Association. (2000). *Diagnostic and Statistical Manual of Mental Disorders. 4th ed.Text revision*. Washington, DC.

Bauman, Z. (2003). *Liquid Love on the Fragility of Human Bonds*. Cambridge: Polity Press.

Bonaparte, M. (1940). Time and the unconscious. *International Journal of Psychoanalysis*, 21: 427–468.

Bowlby, J. *Attachment and Loss. Volume I. Attachment*. New York: Basic Books.

Bowlby, J. (1985). *Separation and Loss. Volume II. Anxiety and Anger*. London: Pelican.

Bowlby J. (1980). *Attachment and Loss Volume III. Sadness and Depression*. New York: Basic Books.

135

Bradley, S.J. (2000). *Affect Regulation and the Development of Psychopathology*. New York: Guilford Press.

Brink, A. (1977). *Loss and Symbolic Repair: A Psychological Study of Some English Poets*. Hamilton, ON: Cromlech Press.

Bronowski, Jacob. (1971). *The Identity of Man*. New York: Natural History Press.

Bronowski, Jacob, (1978). *The Visionary Eye*. Cambridge, MA: MIT Press.

Buber, M. (1970). *I and Thou*. New York: Charles Scribner's Sons.

Buber, M. (1961). *Between Man and Man*. London: Fontana Library.

Camus, A. (1991). *The Myth of Sisyphus*. London: Random House.

Critchley, M. (1979). *Corporeal Awareness: Body Image; Body Scheme in the Divine Banquet of the Brain*. New York: Raven Press.

Csikszentmihalyi, M. (1990). *Flow, the Psychology of Optimal Experience*. New York: HarperCollins.

Davanloo H. (1990). *"Unlocking The Unconscious"*. New York: Wiley.

Deutsch, H. (1942). Some forms of emotional disturbance and their relationship to schizophrenia. *Psychoanalytic Quarterly 11*: 301–321.

Dunlop, Ian. (1977). *Edvard Munch*. London: Thames and Hudson.

Eliot, T.S. (1963). *Collected Poems, 1909–1962. The Centenary Edition*. Orlando, Fl: Harcourt Brace.

Eppel, A.B. (2005). Una visión psicobiológica de la personalidad limítrofe. *Revista de Psiquiatria do Rio Grande do Sul*, *27*: 3.

Eppel, A.B. A psychobiological view of the borderline personality construct. Rev. psiquiatr. Rio Gd. Sul [serial on the Internet]. 2005 Dec [cited 2007 Oct 14] ; 27(3): 262–268. Available from: http://www.scielo.br/scielo.php?script=sci_arttext&pid=S0101–81082005000300005&lng=en&nrm=iso.

Erikson, E. (1950). *Childhood and Society*. New York: W.W. Norton.

Fisher, H. (2004). *Why We Love the Nature and Chemistry of Romantic Love*. New York: Henry Holt.

Fisher, H. (1992). *Anatomy of Love*. New York: Random House.

Fisher, H. & Aron, A. & Brown, L.L. (2005). Romantic love: FMRI study of a neuromechanism for mate choice. *Journal Comp Neurology*, *493* (1): 58–62.

Fitch, S. (2004). *In This House are Many Women*. Fredericton, NB: Goose Lane Editions.

Fonagy, P. (2001). *Attachment Theory and Psychoanalysis*. New York: Other Press.

Fosha, D. (2005). Emotion, True self, true other, Core State; toward a clinical theory of affective change process. *Psychoanalytic Review*, *92*(4): 513–552.

Frankl, V. (2004). *Man's Search for Meaning*. London: Rider.

Freud, S. (1915b). *Thoughts for the Times on War and Death*. Standard Edition.

Freud, S. (1920g). *Beyond the Pleasure Principle*. Standard Edition.

Freud, S. (1930a). *Civilization and Its Discontents*. Standard Edition.

Gallese, V. (2007). Embodies simulation: from mirror neuron systems to interpersonal relations. *Novartis Found Symposium*. 2007; *278*: 3–12.

Gerhardt, S. (2004). *Why Love Matters How Affection Shape a Baby's Brain*. New York: Brunner-Routledge.

Gibran, K. (1978). *The Prophet*. New York: Alfred A. Knopf.

Hendrick, C. & Hendrick, S: (2000). *Close Relationships: A Source Book*. London: Sage Publications.

Jones, E. (1957). *The Life and Work of Sigmund Freud*. New York: Basic Books.

Kandel, E.R. (2006). *In Search of Memory*. New York: W. W. Norton.

Kirkaldie, T.K. & Kitchener, P.D. (2007). When brains expand: mind and the evolution of cortex. *Acta neuropsychiatrica*, *19*(3): 139–148.

Klein, M. (1957). *Envy and Gratitude: A Study of Unconscious Sources*. London: Tavistock Publications.

Lang, F.R., Fingerman, K. L. (2004). *Growing Together Personal Relationships Across the Lifespan*. Cambridge University Press.

Laplanche, J. (1976). *Life and Death in Psychoanalysis*. Baltimore: John Hopkins University Press.

Laplanche, J., Pontalis J.B. (1988). *The Language of Psychoanalysis*. London: Karnac Books.

Lasch, C. (1979). *The Culture of Narcissism. American Life in an Age of Diminishing Expectations*. New York: W. W. Norton.

Lee, J.H. (1973). *The Colours of Love*. Englewood Cliffs, NJ: Prentice Hall.

MacLean, P.D. (1973). *A Triune Concept of the Brain and Behaviour*. Toronto: University of Toronto Press.

Mamet, D. (1992). *Glengarry Glen Ross*: New York: New York: Grove Press.

Mann, J. (1973). *Time Limited Psychotherapy*. Boston: Harvard University Press.

Marcuse, H. (1955). *Eros and Civilization: a Philosophical inquiry into Freud*. Boston: Beacon Press.

Marcuse, H. (1964). *One-Dimensional Man*. Boston: Beacon Press.

Maslow, A. (1970). *Motivation and Personality*. 2nd Ed. New York: Harper and Row.

Maugham, S. (1933). *Sheppey*. London: William Heinemann.

May, R. (1953). *Man's Search for Himself*. New York: Dell Publishing.

Mendelson, M. (1974). *Psychoanalytic Concepts of Depression*. New York: Spectrum Publications.

Nell, V. (2006). Cruelties, Rewards: The Gratifications of Perpetrators and Spectators: Behavioural and Brain Sciences, *29*: 211–257.

O'Neill, E. (1989) *Long Day's Journey into Night*.

Panksepp, J. (1998). *Affective Neuroscience: The Foundations of Human and Animal Emotions*. New York: Oxford University Press.

Panksepp, J., Bernatzky, G. (2002). Emotional sounds and the brain: the neuro-affective foundations of musical appreciation. *Behavioural Processes, 60*(2): 133–155.

Panksepp, J. (2004). *Textbook of Biological Psychiatry*. New Jersey: John Wiley and Sons.

Perel, E. (2006). *Mating in Captivity*. New York: Harper-Collins.

Person, E.S. (2007). *Dreams of Love and Fateful Encounters: The Power of Romantic Passion*. Washington, D.C: American Psychiatric Publishing.

Phillips, A. (1996). *Monogamy*. New York: Vintage Books.

Pine, F. (2004). Mahler's concepts of symbiosis and separation-individuation: Revisited, reevaluated, refined. *Journal of The American Psychoanalytic Association, 52*: 511–533.

Pittman, F. (1989). *Private Lies Infidelity and the Betrayal of Intimacy*. New York: W.W. Norton & Company.

Plath, S. (1981). *The Collected Poems. Harper & Row*.

Roth, P. (1994). *The Professor of Desire*. New York: Vintage Books.

Roth, P. (1994). *Portnoy's Complaint:* New York: Vintage International.

Sartre, J.P. (1989). The Flies. In *Exit and Three Other Plays: The Flies, Dirty Hands, The Respectful Prostitute*. New York: Vintage International.

Schlessinger L. (1995). "Ten Stupid Things Women Do To Mess Up Their Lives". Harper Perennial.

Schore, A.N. (2001). Effects of a secure attachment relationship on right brain development, affect regulation, and infant mental health. *Infant Mental Health Journal, 22*: 7–66.

St. Clair, M. (2000). *Object Relations and Self-Psychology: An Introduction*. 3rd Ed. Belmont, CA: Brooks/Cole, Thompson Learning.

Shakespeare W. (1992). *Romeo and Juliet*. New York: Pocket Books.

Spring, J.A. (1997). *After the Affair: Healing the Pain and Rebuilding Trust When a Partner Has Been Unfaithful.* New York: HarperCollins.

Stuart, H. (2002). Michael Balint: an overview, *American Journal of Psychoanalysis, 62*(1): 37–52.

Sternberg, R.J. (1986). *A Triangular Theory of Love.* Psychological Review 93: 119–135.

Tronick, E. (1998). Dyadically expanded states of consciousness and the process of therapeutic change. *Infant Mental Health Journal, 19*(3): 290–299.

Uddin l, Jacaboni, M., Lange, C., Keenan, J.P. (2007). The self and social cognition: the role of cortical midline structures and the mirror neuron system. *Trends in Cognitive Sciences, 11*(4): 153–157.

Williams, T. (2006). The Milk Train Does Not Stop Here Anymore. In: E.R. Kandel, In Search of Memory. New York: W.W. Norton.

Winnicott, D. (1958). *Collected Papers: Through Paediatrics to Psychoanalysis.* London: Tavistock.

Winnicott, D. (1965). Ego Distortion in Terms of True and False Self in: *The Maturational Processes and the Facilitating Environment.* New York: International Universities Press.

Wolfe, T. (1952). *Look Homeward Angel.* New York: Charles Schibner's sons.

Young L.J., Murphy Young, A.Z., Hammock, E.A.D. (2005). Anatomy and neurochemistry of the pair bond. *Journal Comparative Neurology, 493*(1): 51–57.

INDEX